THE SECRETS OF A

KILLER

AUTO BUSINESS PLAN FOR

SUCCESS

THE SECRETS OF A KILLER AUTO BUSINESS PLAN FOR SUCCESS

DONALD A. FUNK

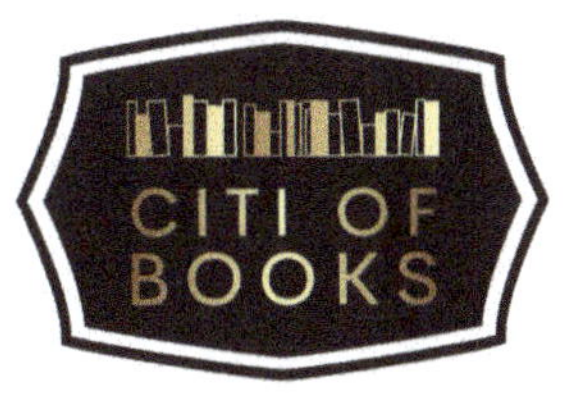

CITIOFBOOKS, INC.
3736 Eubank NE Suite A1
Albuquerque, NM 87111-3579
www.citiofbooks.com
Hotline: 1 (877) 389-2759
Fax: 1 (505) 930-7244

Ordering Information:
Quantity sales. Special discounts are available on quantity purchases by corporations, associations, and others. For details, contact the publisher at the address above.

Printed in the United States of America.

ISBN-13: Softcover 978-1-963209-31-0
eBook 978-1-963209-32-7

Library of Congress Control Number: 2024900844

TABLE OF CONTENTS

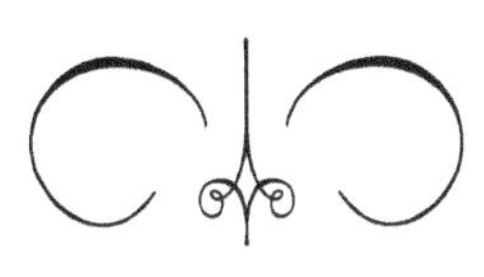

Acknowledgment

I understand that as you grow as an individual on a specific career path, many key people become a part of the process to imprint, impact, influence, inspire, challenge, and motivate you. Many factors shape insights, desires, and passions to continue the journey for a sustainable career with its fulfilling trajectory.

I wish to acknowledge a few individuals with whom I had the distinct privilege of working and they are Ian Van Norman, Dave Deplaedt, and Joe Dand, as well as the many other owners of Canadian Tire that I have consulted with and for over the years. I also had the opportunity to consult and assist many O.E.M. dealers who provided me with further insight into this amazing auto service industry. Likewise, the overall journey has been a stretching and learning experience that was rich and rewarding, causing me to write this fantastic book. As generations come and go, I stand on the shoulders of others within the industry. It has been a thrilling and fantastic ride beyond all telling. I want to share this in-depth insight in an advanced book showing the use of artificial intelligence, smart devices, and a realistic financial business model. This book describes tremendous opportunities to assist the current generation and those that follow on how they can achieve greater potential and opportunities in the future.

Each of the following individuals had a fascinating and unique personality, character traits, and approaches to life and business. They are each very distinguished, true luminaries, and trustworthy individuals.

Ian Van Norman

Ian started his journey to become a self-made man at the age of six when he lost his father in a farming accident. A few years later the family moved to Winnipeg, where he completed his high school education. After graduation, he began his retail career with Zellers in 1955 and continued to work there until 1963, first in Winnipeg, and then transferred to Thunder Bay, Edmonton, Barrie, London, Sarnia, and St. Catharines. In 1963 he was awarded his first Canadian Tire store, #098, in Smiths Falls, Ontario, on a handshake with Mr. A.J. (Alfred) Billis, who, with his two brothers, purchased the Hamilton Tire & Garage Ltd., located in Toronto's Riverdale neighborhood, for $1,800. In 1975 he bought Store #133 in Saskatoon, which he operated for 27 years until retiring in 2002, after 39 incredible years of working in the automotive industry. What a career, and what an amazing individual!

Ian has served his fellow dealers in many capacities and received numerous awards in recognition of his contributions, including the following:

1976 – 1978 Director of CTC
1986 President of Canadian Tire Dealer Association (CTDA)
1990 Director of CTC
1988 Past President of CTDA (and in 1992 – 1993)
Received the Canadian Tire Pace-Setter Award
1992 – 1998 Past Director

1992 – Received the Governor-General's Canadian Caring Award
1996 – Received Dealer Award of Excellence

Ian was also a part of numerous committees, including the Profit Sharing Committee. His wife, Alice, was a significant and integral part of his endeavors and success.

I was honored to be introduced to Canadian Tire on January 2, 1991, by this great gentleman, Ian Van Norman, who invited me to become his auto service manager, where I was until his retirement in 2002. He, along with Alice, was deeply involved with charity projects in Haiti, one of the poorest nations in the world. They built a superb hospital for the Haitian people and offered selfless humanitarian support to this impoverished country. Ian and Alice continued their philanthropic work in Saskatoon and other communities. I was honored to become Mr. Ian Van Norman's automotive service manager, driving the automotive side of the business to new heights, having played a small role in taking the customer service experience to a new level. It has been a great pleasure to know this great individual. He is an amazing businessman who achieved so much, but he was even more remarkable as a genuine friend with whom I had the pleasure of working.

Ian was an extraordinary person of exceptional talent, a great business leader within Canadian Tire, and also built a real estate empire. Still, above all, he was a great man and a special friend. Mr. Van Norman was a world-class person, as was his wife, Alice. They were both great philanthropists.

Dave Deplaedt

I am excited to write a few lines of acknowledgment for this man. Amongst many things, I took note of how focused, disciplined, and extraordinarily organized he was. His daily and weekly calendar (8.5 x 11 with each day underlined) were mapped out in detail: what required his attention, what system needed structure, and what process required improvement. He invested extensively in his upper and middle management team's soft skills and had incredible insight into the importance of structure and accountability. And his follow-up: a one-on-one sit-down to make sure there was execution and delivery. A builder of people, Dave's regular walkabout quickly provided him with a snapshot of what needed attention. He was always super prepared, regardless of whether it was a simple or complicated problem needing attention. He was always open to dialogue and engagement to improve the business, irrespective of the subject. His preparations led to greater success. With an outlook like that, I quickly realized how he always maximized the opportunities before him. Many great leaders spread themselves thin – so thin they probably should have cloned themselves if possible. Dave is the Leader of Leaders, the best-of-the-best operators, a Guru of all things Canadian Tire, indispensable to those within the dealers' group and within the corporation. He is a talented, sought-after individual. Yet, after twenty-plus years, Dave Deplaedt has tirelessly volunteered his time for the betterment of his fellow dealers and the corporation. His tremendous workload, and the many hats he continues to wear, are impressive, to say the least.

Lastly, Dave's philanthropic involvement in the community is exceptional, such as the charity golf tournament he initiated for the benefit of the Saskatoon Food Bank, a fantastic fundraiser that grows every year and has provided millions for this worthy cause.

Dave Deplaedt was a great dealer to work with and for. At all times we were on the same philosophical page at the end of our many conversations, planning strategies for the next level of achievement. Our collective achievement was incredible. Every day the ride was exhilarating. Dave is a fantastic dealer and super-organized, with a ton of smarts. "Brilliant" would be the best term to describe this individual and friend.

As for recognition, he received the CTDA Heavy Lifter Award and CTC Award of Excellence in 2008. Here is the chronology of his CTC/ CTDA involvement:

DEALER ASSOC., DEALER GROUP, DEALER HOLDINGS, OTHER COMMITTEES

Group	Dates	Position
GTAA	1998-2000	MAC Automotive
OVDA/Mid Canada	2000-2003	MAC Automotive/ NSC
Mid-Canada	2003-2005	MAC Chair Automotive/AOC
Mid-Canada	2005-2007	CTDA Director
Mid-Canada	2007-2011	AI Chair
Mid-Canada	2011-2014	CTDA President
Mid-Canada	2014- current	Contract Comm & Point Team

Joe Dand

Joe Dand was the youngest Vice President hired at Canadian Tire, as well as the youngest dealer to receive the "Dealer Award of Excellence." Joe always had the knack to manage a successful turnaround and has been very prosperous in many other business endeavors. A great individual to work for and with. Together, we achieved remarkable and monumental success in building the auto service side into the top echelons while joining the elites on the service side.

Ryan Jago

I am extremely privileged and honored to have been introduced to this individual who wanted a job to pay for his schooling at the University of Saskatchewan. In those early days, he had some health issues, but to his credit, he battled through, turning the corner to better health. During this time, I was promoting another assistant service manager at Store #133, a Canadian Tire store. I approached Ryan to see if he would be interested in serving as the assistant service manager. I challenged Ryan, who was always pushing the envelope, to consider becoming a Canadian Tire Dealer in the future. Within days, I received an extremely well-written letter (of which I still have a copy) saying yes. Ryan, you are well on your way to becoming a great Dealer, and I look forward to seeing you excel.

Dr. Eleanor Funk

This dear person has been a tremendous partner and individual, and more importantly, the most remarkable wife and soulmate one could imagine. Without her precious involvement, this project may have never been completed.

She has been a highly capable, helpful individual and a great encourager and assistant. To my wife, Eleanor, for her love, support, patience, friendship, and, above everything else, the strength she gave to this project (and all the other ones), she can only be described as remarkable.

Final Thrilling Thoughts

I have had so many thrilling moments, thanks to Ian Van Norman and Dave Deplaedt, who crossed the threshold of greatness by receiving the "Dealer of Excellence Award," in addition to other well-deserved recognitions over the years.

There have been many others, too, like Dave Malcomson and Adam Stuart, who had no or little auto experience. Dave Malcomson first reached out to me while I was still working with Dave Deplaedt and helped me launch my successful auto consulting career. He had a very good store and auto service department that attracted a new team member who was both intelligent and well-educated. His name was Adam Stewart, and he had a great passion and desire to take the business to a new level and, in a short time, achieved the status of an iconic Service Manager with his many achievements.

After just two weeks, Adam's and Dave's auto service took off like that of a successful launch of a rocket, culminating in an incredible story of achievement in the ensuing years – one that Adam will continue in the future. Thanks to Dave for reaching out to me to launch my career as a trusted auto service consultant who then helped many stores transition from being good to elite. On December 13, 2009, just before my career move to Auto Service Consultant, I received a notice from Dave Deplaedt that four of the top five Canadian Tire corporate executives were flying out to meet in the board room of Store #133. They were Mike Medline, Allan MacDonald, Mike Walsh, and Peter Kilty. This visit was to see how they could share the continued sales growth concepts, strategies, and best practices to facilitate progress in the coming years. Another individual I greatly appreciated was Michael Ferris, the VP of Canadian Tire Auto Service.

We had discussions about my joining his team. I believe it would have been a very rewarding experience, but, unfortunately, the timing was not right, and it would have been a step backward for me from the benefits of doing consultations. However, I enjoyed the time I spent with him, and when Mike became the dealer in Midland, Ontario, I enjoyed spending time at his store just as much.

The biggest room in the auto service industry is the room for improvement in connecting with consumers to deliver a high level of customer service experience, and as a result, locking them in as clients for life. Customers are the currency that pays all your bills. In this challenging field, one can indeed build a truly rewarding "trust economy." This book provides those secrets.

"A lot of times, people Do not know what they want until you show it to them."

- Steve Jobs

FOREWORD

Five decades in the auto repair and service business have been an amazing experience for me. I have enjoyed the various stages, challenges, and opportunities of taking a company to the very top. Over these long years, I have learned that companies must adapt to change – that is what drives opportunity – and, if You are passionate about this remarkable industry, You will never work a day in your life. My goal and vision are to assist organizations and individuals in reaching their apex potential, which, in most cases, is unlimited. I know they can thrive with the right insight, training, secrets, common sense, ideas, concepts, and vision to seize the opportunities, which create a new business success journey.

I want to go on record with straightforward insights, diving deep into the industry without spin or fluffy approaches that push painful issues under the carpet. To remove that pain and frustration, we must tackle those issues with a head-on approach at times, flat-out owning our problems and resolving them by asking for input. Keep in mind: the long view is not based on current issues and problems. Look at real long-term potential, perhaps ten years out, and factor this into a bigger picture. The opportunities are vast and unlimited. Over my five-decade-long career, I attended numerous training seminars, and webinars, spoke with some of the best consultants and countless other sources in North America, and visited many conventions to absorb as much information as possible. I also researched the industry's best contributors to understand what is new, what is changing, and what is cutting edge, and while writing this self-help road map to success (top-line and bottom-line), I spent endless hours reading, and investigating a wide range of subjects, studies, and thorny issues, to be as relevant as possible.

Specific articles and documents I found are right on the mark. As I am standing on their shoulders, I desire to thank and credit them for their gifted writing and research. The marketplace and culture are changing rapidly, so this book is intended to provide some necessary cerebral content that will make a certain percentage of readers think. It outlines a plethora of processes, best practices, logic, and training/education check MARKS (versus check POINTS), revisiting customer service to reduce customer churn. Research into particular subjects has armed me with many revelations and provided rich content. I recognize that someone has to take this industry forward and realize its true potential. Within this document, I will be sharing a great deal of that gold. Do not just sell. Instead, educate the consumer, so they truly and clearly understand what is in it for *them*, thus selling it to *themselves*. Sound, substantial value is what motivates buyers to pay for excellent, amazing products and services.

No one wants to be sold.

The more effective approach is to educate and build personal relationships that are relevant and authentic, so you are assisting the consumers in the buying process. You have to learn how to remove pain and friction, so they are delighted and become evangelists of your brand on your behalf and spread their gospel message for free.

It is still the best form of advertising out there and leads to a lot more "Yes" from the customers. Vehicles will always require service and repair. The manufacturers will still recommend that owners follow engineers' preventative maintenance interval schedules to extend their products' life cycles and keep them re-investing in their brands. In many ways, the auto service industry is undergoing a thinking renaissance. Customer service is (or should be) coming into its own as a specialty, offering consumers an experience that most competitors will have great difficulty in replicating. Adaptation is necessary. Study after study reveals excessive amounts of consumer and employee churn. After five years, 87% of new car buyers abandon their dealership's service department when their warranty expires. Of the remaining 13%, some will die or relocate, so the share of the pie becomes even smaller.

As your role evolves, the need is paramount for a better and more effective range of soft skill sets to communicate – and not just at entry-level positions. Talented customer service professionals need a tremendous operating knowledge of the industry and, more importantly, an effective method of delivering that knowledge. You require staff to educate consumers so they understand what that system does, what the benefits are, and what value it offers. Educate and extend their awareness of the manufacturer's preventative maintenance interval schedules, which are designed to increase the life cycle of their product as well as the enjoyment attached to their vehicle, which helps sell the next one. Again, customer service traction must be won by offering a fantastic experience, which is vital in maintaining continuous growth. Focus on honing a skill set built for customer retention and loyalty.

After nearly five decades in this industry, I wrote this book for businesses and staffers to help them build and grow valuable customer service for use in world-class training teams that will execute that better service experience. I wrote it to create awareness of what is required to win a larger piece of hundreds of billions of dollars of opportunities that are up for grabs. Churn data and studies confirm that the opportunity is real.

The industry is still evolving through a period of tumult, where consumers continually seek a better experience from the front-line advisors who are the face and voice of your business. It is about taking your team – everyone – on a new journey.

More is always better.

There Is No Room for Anything Less than Excellence

The quality of your customer service will never exceed the quality of the people providing it.

Your Front Line Builds Your Bottom Line.

The question is, how to get your staff to buy in? I believe one has to create a new cultural incentive program built around rewards and recognition programs that inspire and challenge everyone to be a part of this unlimited opportunity. As Lexus says:

"Service is not just a department. It is not a sign hanging on the wall. It is a commitment. To be helpful. To be compassionate. To treat people like guests. It is what we all signed up for. And every day, we wake up and rededicate ourselves to it. During the good times and bad, when we take care of people first, the rest will follow."

During my five-decade career, I had the privilege to touch countless people by investing in them.

I took endless time to imprint, impact, coach, mentor, motivate, provide wisdom, and challenge my team members to develop soft skill sets and industry knowledge so they could become more than they ever dreamed possible. I encourage them that what we see ahead of us might seem impossible, but with effort and commitment, everything is possible.

There were times of failure in my career too, which were great lessons to learn from. Later on, reflecting on these mistakes and then learning from them made me realize the importance of team building. It was amazing, beyond words. Everyone who trusted me, I put great effort into proving them right and did what others considered the impossible.

Another privilege was to service those "very special guests who would grace our doors." That is how I knew investing in others was the ultimate means to retain the guests who shared their wallets. This rich experience gave me a passion for writing about the industry and how we can better accommodate others to learn valuable insights and learn to better accommodate others.

It is my desire for each individual to enrich and reward themselves by providing a higher quality customer service experience. To earn more, you have got to become more! This applies to everyone: the CEO, owner, parts manager, service manager, service advisor, techs, and apprentices.

The research and the writing that went into composing this book expanded the insight that I gained over these five decades. It has allowed me to claim the proud title of being one of the most read individuals in these amazing, exciting, and passionate areas of Auto Service.

Title: Mr. Encyclopedia of Auto Service.

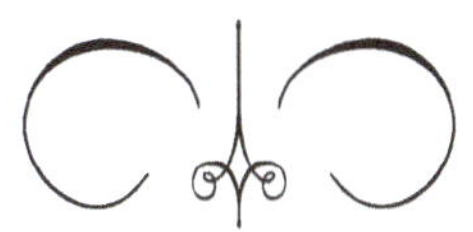

About the Author

Don Funk Profile

Belonging to cosmopolitan Saskatchewan, with his primary education received from Lanigan Central High School, Lanigan, Don Funk comes from a very respectable family and has a diploma in Business Management and a certificate in Automotive Journeyman, both from NAIT, Edmonton, Alberta. He has also taken Disney's course on Leadership Excellence and Business Marketing. Don Funk is an experienced individual and the absolute best when it comes to auto-service consulting.

Professional Career:

Don Funk has had an impressive career that spans more than 52 years. Initially, between 1965 to 1971, he was employed at **Bill's Ag Semi-Truck and Auto-Service Center** and **Lo-Cost Automatic Transmission**, with locations in Saskatoon, Edmonton, Victoria, and Calgary. In 1972, he became the owner and operator of **All-O-Matic Transmission** which he sold later on in 1990. From 1991 till 2009, Don was employed as the service manager of **Canadian Tire #133,** which went on to become the #1 store out of approximately 500 stores in all of Canada, volume-wise, due to its outstanding customer service. Lastly, he started and ran his consulting firm, **Funk Auto-Service Consulting**, from 2009 until 2019. Don Funk is also the author of *Mr. Encyclopedia of Auto Service*.

Community Involvement

Don was the VP of the **Saskatchewan Worker's Compensation Safety Program** (1990–2001) and **Saskatchewan Scrap Tire Corporation** (1998–2009) in Regina, Saskatchewan. He was the board director of the **Saskatchewan Automotive Apprentice Board** in 2006 and a board member of the **Saskatchewan Sports Hall of Fame and Museum Board** from 1998 to 2006. He also served as a board director at the **Alliance Senior Care Home** for three years. Later on, he was elected to the **Saskatoon Sports Hall of Fame**, and **Saskatchewan Sports Hall of Fame**, in the 'Builder' category, in 2004 and 2007, respectively.

In 1987, Don prepared a bid for the **International Softball Congress** and hosted 48 club teams from around the world, attracting a record 100,000-plus softball fans. In the following year, he again prepared a bid for the **International Softball Federation** and hosted teams from 14 countries from around the world. Both of these events were the first-ever attempts to host such events in the history of softball in Canada, and Don Funk co-chaired both these events. Once again, a record number of countries participated, and record gate receipts and attendance were received, with over 100,000-plus in attendance.

In 1980, Don Funk sponsored the **Saskatchewan Rick Folk Curling** team that won the Canadian Championship in Calgary and the World Curling Championship in Moncton. He was appointed **Chef de Mission**, representing Softball Canada at the Argentina trials (1981) and **The World Congress** in Japan (1986). He served as commissioner (Western Canada) with **International Softball Canada** as director of Canada's national men's teams – director and junior programs on the international level (1991–1993).

Don Funk has nominated (and, as a result, were elected) worthy individuals in the community compiled their many outstanding accomplishments and achievements, and presented them to the following: Order of Canada (2); Canada's Sports Hall of Fame (2); Walk of Fame Toronto; 10 or more to Saskatchewan Sports Hall of Fame & Museum in Regina; 10 to the Saskatoon Sports Hall of Fame; and 5 sports teams. Together with his wife, Dr. Eleanor Funk, he raised approximately 10 million dollars in community events.

Government Recognition

Numerous awards have been awarded to Don Funk over the years. He was the recipient of the **Award of Excellence** with the Certificate of Merit from the government of Canada for his contribution to the community in 1998. He received recognition and was honored by the province of Saskatchewan as **a Goodwill Ambassador**. He has also been honored by the city of Saskatoon with the naming of **Funk Park** in the **Evergreen Community** for promoting the city of Saskatoon – provincially, nationally, and internationally (2016).

Involvement in Faith Community

Don Funk was the associate chairman, in the year 1995, of the **Franklin and Billy Graham Crusade**, with over 100,000 (over 4 days) in attendance, (plus 4 satellite feeds), and the Saskatchewan ambassador for **Haggai Institute**. This institute helps equip and train indigenous world leaders in 189 countries who, in turn, become ambassadors to further evangelize effective leaders for the kingdom's work, become effective and influential leaders to their governments when a crisis hits within their borders and work with governments to end corruption.

He was the director of **Campus Crusade**, provincially and nationally, by rebranding the name to 'Power to Change.' This was a month-long program that involved the entire faith community in all areas of the province. Don was involved with the media across the province to complete the rebrand.

Don was the chairman for the annual **Saskatoon Mayor's Prayer Breakfast** (2004–2016), where they invited leaders as speakers who were known within Canada and around the world. An example was a couple of the 33 Chilean miners who were in the tomb for 67 days. During this timeframe, they drew up to 2,500 people per meeting who came out to hear them firsthand.

His wife, Dr. Eleanor Funk, president of **Hebrew Tabernacle Reproduction Society Inc.**, and Don have been in the ministry for 40 years, and, in the year 2020, they built a permanent life-size model of the Tabernacle of Moses near Rosthern, Saskatchewan, the only life-size permanent Tabernacle of Moses model in Canada. Don and Eleanor have worked with **Intervarsity** as a host family for the international fellowship of foreign students, helping students adjust to life in Canada in many different settings. They have been involved with the church for all of their lives and love the word of God (also a Gideon's representative – Northern Saskatchewan).

Don and Eleanor Funk have hosted and chaired **The Mayor's Prayer Breakfasts** in Saskatoon for 12 years while bringing news-worthy guest speakers from around the world, for example:

- A doctor from Argentina who performed the first three of four heart transplants.
- The 32 miners from Chile were trapped in a mine 2,300 feet below ground in what was almost a tomb, for 67 days, with little food that was rationed.

At one of these breakfasts, the Funks honored six people and their families: four soldiers from Saskatchewan, who lost their lives in Afghanistan, and two RCMPs, one in a stand-off and another on the highway. They had set a record for the largest meal reception in the province, with invitations sent to all three levels of government and the First Nations. Up to as many as 2,600 folks attended each of these events/breakfasts.

Don and Eleanor Funk were recognized with **Certificate Appreciation Presented by Saskatoon Police:** "In appreciation and recognition for the sincere and gracious duties you performed in bringing the Saskatoon Police Service and its provincial protection-service partners together for the first Memorial Service.

Your professional and kind actions have made us all feel and recognize our communities' appreciation for men and women who 'serve to protect'". In friendship, Dave Scott Chief of Police, April 21, 2001

Don Funk's trademark has always been to invest in his staff and develop the talent and skillsets for success while continuing to challenge them to become superstars. One has to be an architect to build and hold staff accountable in providing a hallmark-quality customer-service experience, which is second to none, thus earning the 'Top Score' of 'Extremely Satisfied' or 'Most Definitely Will Return' review. Constant coaching in the future development of the next generation of the talent industry is the key to success. Become a 'Hall of Famer' by educating and empowering people with knowledge.

"For everyone to whom much is given, from him, much will be required."

Luke 12:24

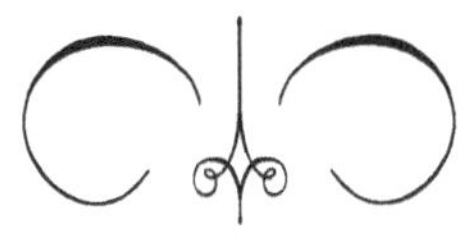

Chapter 1

Creating an Incredible 'Disney-like' Customer Experience

"A great leader is a teacher and a coach, not a dictator."

–Ashira Prossack

Elevated Leadership

"I believe in being a motivator."

–Walt Disney

Elevated leadership is about empowering people to lead with purpose, vision, and influence to enable greatness in themselves and others. Every business in the country wants to grow its customer base. This chapter nails it. The business dynamics of the world and the marketplace are ever-changing. Strategies and methods are constantly evolving. What worked for a business a decade ago might not necessarily be applicable in today's age for the same business.

For better comprehension, think of it as survival in a very competitive industry. In the USA, 2.2 million vehicles are brought in every day for repair and maintenance service. If you want to outperform your competitors, you must take the customer service experience to a whole new level. You must flat-out make that experience memorable with an incredible 'Disney-like' experience to make the consumer happy. That is where the process must begin. One must deliver service with a genuine touch that is completely relevant in today's very competitive marketplace. You must pay attention to every aspect so you can grab every opportunity there is and deliver the most promising services to your customer. Many businesses are flourishing with positive change despite having competitors. The present times require you to stay one step ahead and level up your game if your aim is to leave behind the competition. This requires every cast member to be on board while delivering their very best 100% of the time.

The magic has to come from within you and the entire team by making the consumer's experiences your number one priority. This requires 100% buy-in from the entire front and back-end cast members. You can never take your eyes off the prize, i.e., the consumer; they are the VIPs (very important people) that allow every check to be written, including yours. You must remove all the pain points and kick the 'ugly churn monster' to the curb and lock him out. This makes life so much easier. Consumers are willing to share their wallets time and time again, and when you excel in customer service with the goal to please, they are willing to pay more for a high and greater level of service, and especially when you create value: that is the consumers' hot button. Here is the secret: **you must over-deliver the customer service experience,** thereby having them become an evangelist for your brand. 69 % of the consumers said that they look up reviews on their smart devices while shopping in a store, and 53 % said they search for deals before asking an employee, according to a 'RetailMeNot' study.

Thus, every interaction needs to be calculated and effectively communicated with your audience. Educate to empower them and allow them to decide what they want to buy, as knowledge is power. Customers are more knowledgeable these days and are not easily deceived into buying products and services they do not want or feel they need.

They make more informed choices now, so all the power is placed in the hands of the customer. Smart devices, especially in the automotive service business, take your customer service experience to the next level, without a doubt. With the increasing competition in the marketplace, generating one-time sales is not enough. You need to leave a lasting impression on your customers to develop a loyal clientele that will keep coming back for more. How do you do that? How do you win over clients? The answer is simple: all the focus needs to be on your clients. You need to make them feel like they are special and that they truly matter. So, I suggest you take these ideas, insights, and inspirations into your business. You need to show them that you and your business care for them more than any other business out there. Customer service needs to be exceptional to achieve that goal. You need to go the extra mile to make your customers feel greatly appreciated.

Creating and maintaining a good product is not enough; delivering high-quality yet concise and precise communication in a way that is impactful and memorable is essential. Not only must it convert a prospect into a loyal customer, it must also make them want to become an evangelist for your brand of their own accord. Adding an element of surprise would help elevate your customer's experience, and they will leave your service center satisfied. If you can think on your feet, and with the right comment, you can make the consumer's day - big time! Putting in the extra effort with even the smallest of words and the tiniest of actions can make a huge difference in making a client feel valued and appreciated. Business is a two-way street in which building a personalized relationship with the client that is authentic and relevant retains long-term trust and respect that will go a long way for your brand. No matter how good your advertising is, no amount or quality of advertisements can beat the recommendation of a satisfied customer. People are well-educated and well-informed these days, and they look to others for honest reviews before seeking any new product or service. According to a study, 88% of consumers are willing to pay more for a better product and exemplary service experience.

Use the power of social media. Ask for a Facebook like. Client reviews can make or break a business. A recent study has revealed that clients who find your business through referrals are likely to spend 200% more on your business than other customers. You, as a team, need to earn and own the magic of the service moment by adding a little pixie dust! It is simple, as thoughtful and kind words or the little extra effort gets them going.

Whether it is the production, marketing, sales, or post-sales phase, you need to interact with your customers every step of the way to let them know that they are your number one priority, always. To do that, you need to re-evaluate your entire business model. Identify the department and cast members in charge of catering to the clientele and ensure that it is an outstanding and memorable moment(s). Apart from the actual product, good customer service is what clients want and are even willing to pay more for. Customer service is the key to staying ahead of the competition. The reason many businesses fall behind is that they become stagnant over time by failing to keep an eye on the prize, which, in this case, is a consumer. A 2015 Aspect Consumer Experience Survey revealed that 76% of consumers believe the quality of customer service they receive is the most accurate indicator of how much a business values them. That shows how imperative a good customer service experience is for the overall success of a business.

"Whatever you do, do it well. Do it so well that when people see you do it, they will want to come back and see you do it again, and they will want to bring others and show them how well you do what you do."

–Walt Disney

Those are the words of Walt Disney, whose vision led to the creation of Disney World, which is famous all around the globe for its exceptional customer service. 'Guestology,' a term coined at Disney, is one of the most widely accepted customer service theories today. Guestology involves understanding and anticipating the expectations and needs of potential customers and fulfilling those needs before they even realize or ask for them. Guestology means 'the study of guests.' The reason the customer service (referred to as guest service by Disney) at Disney is known all around the world is that they treat each one of their customers as a guest and provide excellent, personalized, and professional customer service in all areas of the business. Whether you are visiting for the first time or the tenth time, you are treated the same way as a special guest. Businesses can study how Disney works and make notes of their own to improve their brand.

According to Disney, a fantastic experience relies on the excellence of leadership. Good leadership can help every individual in an organization identify their roles and responsibilities to provide customer support accordingly.

At Disney, the cast members (employees) follow a set of standards that guide them through decision-making processes to resolve issues quickly and help them feel empowered. You can do this by holding training sessions for your employees and providing them with the necessary tools, including word tracks and information about your brand. Reward employees for their hard work to motivate them and further increase their productivity. Provide them a space to share their creative inputs to develop a sense of ownership by employees, which will make them more honest and dedicated toward their work. Apply the 4Rs rule to your team – reinforce, reset, revisit, reapply. Keep going over strategies and processes to ensure these rules are in practice and be sure to keep all team members in the loop. Caring for employees and making them feel valued will result in them caring for the customers in the same way. It is about breeding a new culture of care for all. It is about modeling partnerships with all the cast members for greater rewarding results.

Think of your business as the best place where customers are treated as guests. Identify key elements that will magnify the customer experience. Pay attention to all the details. What changes would you make to accommodate your guests? Stop at nothing; pull all the stops necessary; leave nothing unturned. What are their likes and dislikes? What can be done to make the guests' experience better? Examine every detail and interaction and learn to deliver it in a seamless manner.

What will make your business stand out in the minds of the guests? These are some things you need to think about to gain valuable insights and to be able to improve the customer experience. Do not just stick to these basic things; think outside the box. What is one thing that you associate with Disney? Creativity. Creativity is golden, so is the magic of the moment, and you will find that it is very rewarding. Everyone has a spark of creativity in them; it just needs to be brought out to the surface so your talent and personality can shine. I want to encourage you to purchase the book '*How to be Like Walt*.' I want you to explore and further whet your appetite. Do it, and it will change your career and life. To do that, you must remember the *Disney box.* The four corners of the box symbolize your vision (what you want to be), your mission (what you want to achieve), the customer (the person you are building the experience for), and the essence (what to feel).

Businesses today, although successful, lack the dynamism that you see in Disney. That is because all businesses have adapted the same models. Everyone is doing the same thing, which results in business practices becoming stagnant. Creating an environment that encourages creativity produces good ideas that can be beneficial for the business and drive everyone involved into leveling up their game.

What else does Disney do that sets them apart from every other business? On top of fulfilling the physical and functional needs of customers, they focus on emotional needs as well. They have made that emotional connection. Over the years, they have introduced cruise liners and Disney-land weddings to their list of services because they realized that was what the clients wanted. This was achieved because Disney knew that listening to the client was the best source of information. To Disney, a customer is more than a means to an end – a customer is a guest, and guestology is the key to winning them over.

Always strive to do something unique, something that will exceed the customer's expectations and something that they will never forget. When customers get more than they expected, it is like a pleasant surprise for them, and who does not like surprises? These surprises help create an impact. Make it an event, unleash the magic of the moment, be gracious, and consider it a privilege to serve. Taking steps to enhance a customer's experience makes you stand out from other brands and helps establish goodwill with customers.

Another secret of Disney's success is that they form strong, long-term relationships with the customers. Re-elevate all the tiny details, take the time to get to know your customer and understand them. Build a personalized, lasting relationship of trust with customers who are loyal and can become advocates for your business and, thus, promote your brand.

Timothy Ferriss once said, *"Information is useless if it is not applied to something important or if you will forget it before you have a chance to apply it."* Information is what dominates every domain of the world today. Make use of your tools and gather as much information as you can. Use social media to promote your business and collect data. Introduce surveys, conduct polls, and ask for reviews. Ask the consumer to give a like on Facebook and other social media platforms. You can also offer rewards for customers who promote your products or services.

There are several sources to analyze and identify the particular needs of customers, but perhaps the best of all is customer feedback.

Feedback is more important and valuable than all other forms of information gathering because it is more personal and shows you up close what the client thinks of your business. In addition to that, it provides you with valuable insights about the current customer experience and what departments are lacking.

Besides relying on feedback, Disney also relies on the cast members' observation skills to further improve customer experience. For example, cast members realized that disabled individuals often got frustrated at different locations because they had to constantly inform the cast members of their disability. Disney then created "special assistance" passes for disabled guests and provided special training to the staff to identify and fulfill the needs of these disabled guests. Hence, you have to transform your customer service by providing an amazing experience that exceeds the customer expectation 100% by having cast members execute the service with kind, appreciating words and meaningful and thoughtful actions.

There are many ways of collecting data in this day and age, but the important question is, how do you use that data to your advantage? So, let us examine these steps. The first step of leading any business is to know your target audience. With all the information available to you, you can partake in customer profiling in which you can create prototypes of potential clients and predict their wants, needs, and desires. For every group of individuals, you can predict their likes and dislikes and create scenarios that appeal to them all.

Once you have established that, you can follow Disney's way of delivering customer service; they are the guiding light. They rely on three things; the cast, setting, and process. For your business, the cast would be the employees, the setting would be the platform you are using to interact with your clients, and the process would be the solid strategies you utilize to deliver personalized experiences to your customers. This is a winning business formula, as proven by Disney, and will allow you to stay ahead of your competitors. Customers are running the show now. Incorporating customer feedback into customer experience results in a strategy that enhances the overall customer experience and satisfies customers. Since one-time sales are insufficient for the success of a business now, it is essential to remember that the actual sale begins **after** the sale. With consistent and predictable customer service, you can make customers come back time and time again for more. When you are doing it right, with a little over-the-top experience, you win the day.

As the consumers love it, they want to come back and see you do it again. Still, if you only focus on getting them to the point of sale, your efforts will mean very little, and you will have failed to make the event memorable, like that of your experience of going to Disney to refresh the real Disney-like experience. Every business must rethink its strategy; your focus must be on the process – Process drives everything and is the backbone of all the details. The magic of the moment comes when one has perfected the process, thus, achieving quality.

Your focus and effort should delight consumers if you did exceedingly well. If the customer asks or requests something, your response should be, *"Absolutely!"* Your primary goal is to create the magic of the memorable moment of happiness, the little moment(s) where you focus entirely on your guests. Leaders at Disney are constantly teaching about the customer experience for each cast member to create magical moments. It is about equipping and empowering them to enhance the guest experience that makes the difference. As cast members, when having interactions, you have to create a little magic of owning the service as you create that emotional connection. If you have the knowledge and confidence, you let your personality shine. That is where the magic comes from, through the gracious tone of your voice and your body language while creating those special magical moments.

At Disney, it is about acting, and they teach you how to perform; all of you can act and, with a little extra work, polish these moments on your own stage, fuss over the guest, and make their day. It is about the feeling, the smile, that connection of creating your own magic. If you do it with taste and sincerity, That is the 'tell' of a magical moment. When the customer lights up social media by boasting, it provides thc opportunity for others to come and experience the same magic!

With the help of 'The Secret of an 'Auto Killer Business Plan," all of you can earn the ultimate customer experience by applying the strategies and processes discussed here for the success of your business and to own the true magic of the moment. You will be able to create something very special for yourself. As a leader, engage your cast members and create a new vision. You can takc your tcam on an exciting journey and enhance your enterprise by taking it to the elite level for greater success.

A study measured the satisfaction and intended loyalty among owners of vehicles that are 4–12 years old and analyzed the customer experience in both warranty and non-warranty service visits. Overall, satisfaction was based on five factors (in order of importance): service initiation (24%), service quality (23%), service advisor

(20%), service facility (17%), and vehicle pick-up (16%). As a side note, initiation is the beginning of a process, which is very important.

Effective communication is essential to increasing satisfaction, J.D. Power observed.

It is about orchestrating the customer journey in these five areas, which will significantly improve and manage the customer expectations.

Initiation is the beginning of a process that is very formal (professional) with attention to all the details. So, again, it is about engaging, educating to empower, and executing the necessary and important final step, the 'Ask' for the business. You need to consider the five engaging steps. With the execution of the five steps, You will be on the way to greater success. After all, it begins with excellence in delivery!

"Do a good job. You do not have to worry about the money; it will take care of itself. Just do your best work then try to trump it."

–Walt Disney

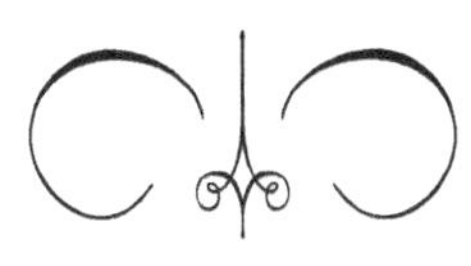

CHAPTER 2

SETTING THE PACE FOR GREATER SUCCESS

"I like the impossible because there is less competition."

–Walt Disney

The secret of a killer business plan is that it must be built on the core values that have been tested and proven over time. These core values have to begin with delivering and embedding an amazing, high-level customer service experience. This is the true secret to greater success.

This book will change your entire outlook by expanding your business and personal growth. It will also drive your business with a growth cycle so that all shops and service centers will go from being 'average' to 'good' and from 'good' to 'elite' service centers. Without question, the elite centers can be fine-tuned if they shift their focus to three major KPIs, which include generating consistent new traffic, resulting in an explosion of sales, while closely monitoring and controlling expenses which will result in stronger margins to the bottom line. That is exciting stuff! However, the second tell-tale sign of success is managing the labor cost since this critical piece contributes to control versus sales and generates a margin of 30%

and well beyond. This is a critical step in management; the better service centers understand that on any day in the week, one can quickly calculate and know the percentage of sales minus the labor costs. It is about efficiencies and productivity. Have the right mix between journeymen or accredited technicians and apprentices at various stages, i.e., oil and lube techs. If you cannot measure it…you cannot manage it, and what gets measured gets done.

The secret is controlling all the other related expenditures. Each expense is required to be reviewed, re-evaluated, and requoted to control these costs; thus, meeting the goals and objectives is about shaping the bottom line to have a positive impact. However, this is often overlooked. With this insight, even the 20/80 rule will experience an exciting new growth curve from 20 to 100%. A plethora of opportunities can be generated by applying this great insight.

The objective of this book is to direct your focus toward operational excellence to maximize new growth traffic cycles (deliver an elevated customer experience) year after year, thus multiplying sales exponentially year in and year out and driving and expanding the margins worth your effort and energy while squeezing value out of your current assets, making the banker smile and congratulate your efforts. However, it has to be ethical in nature. The amazing and incredible Disney-like customer experience is the driver of new and repeated business; That is the number one reason for consumers falling in love with a world-class brand experience. When executed right with that special touch, consumers are impressed and are over-the-top about it on social media. A memorable customer service experience generates new footsteps; it is critical to convert consumers into being an evangelist for your brand, as they can help influence many others to become raving fans.

When it comes to preventative maintenance, it should always be recommended. Printing off the manufacturer's service interval schedule based on the consumer's mileage and explaining the 'WIIFM' (What is in It For Me) and presenting this powerful printed document influences the consumer's choice. By presenting the maintenance schedule, based on mileage, along with sharing and then educating the consumer about the amazing benefits and incredible values, helps motivate the consumer into realizing what is in it for them. Often, the next question is, 'When can it be ready?' or, 'What is the cost of the service?' Another tip is packaging two or three services together. Value causes the consumer to willingly share their wallets and lock them in without the grudge of high-pressure selling. Education is powerful and effective which is the third secret formula for greater $uccess in providing the ultimate customer experience.

Another secret in driving sales is overcoming objections (another great opportunity to convert a prospect into a consumer), which can be your best friend in increasing your sales. Chapter 10 is all about unlocking the Secrets to Overcoming Objections and Winning. This later chapter will show how to capitalize on the closing percentage by understanding and implementing these secrets.

Now, the question which often arises is, what is a reasonable timeframe in which to expect a payback on investing in new equipment such as the amazing Hunter Engineering Quick Check Alignment? The answer is, in months (three to four), depending on the traffic you generate, but certainly in year one. Google Hunter Engineering and ask them to give you a quote based on your annual traffic. The payback is almost always dependent on the manager's insight and experience of being a visionary leader. For the larger percent of service managers, the payback should be quick, showing a positive and amazing change within months or a one-year window at the latest. Many auto centers are completely pumped and quickly realize that the data obtained from AutoServe1 is rock solid. In fact, it sells itself. However, an initial training session can help all technicians, regardless of their experience, have a comfort level and confidence in the power of these smart tools. Such equipment will bring about confidence, accountability, encouragement, and support for a consumer that will further bring an additional lifetime of rewards to your enterprise. This will lock them in; That is how impressive it is. You can bank on this investment in AI, as it will generate another exciting and extended growth cycle that will drive the three major KPI's right through the roof.

During my consultant career, I had a week-long session with an auto service store, a top quartile store in the city of Calgary, Alberta, whereby I did a deep dive into the operation. During the week, we focused on breaking down old habits; after that, the next goal was to establish time-tested and proven processes, with a refresher course, which led to a solid 30% gain. At the end of my week there, the C.E.O. of this chain store asked me if I could return whenever I had an open week. In my experience, and certainly in my role as a consultant, I have learned that one needs to bring an element of change. Change, however, comes bearing its own challenges. This is why you need to breed a new culture, the one that cast members are unable to resist, and which allows them to visualize the new opportunities that this change will be bringing.

What Can We Learn from Disney's Experience and History?

Walt Disney was bold, innovative, and creative in the characteristics that he used as a vehicle to drive change that brought about a happy and satisfying customer experience for all ages going forward. Thus, your approach must be impeccable, relentless, and memorable. I wanted to provide a glimpse into the world of Disney because you cannot take customer service for granted. It is the key to greater success, as being average at CSI will not lead your business anywhere.

The amazing secrets must capture the customer's imagination and create magical moments, so they can add to the experience that must be memorable indeed, like being at an exciting event. The advanced customer service experience sets the stage for consumers with a Disney-like atmosphere delivered by cast members who are going all out to provide impressive magical moments by pulling all the stops in winning the consumer over for a lifetime; That is the secret: bigger payback! Leadership is the key, and constant coaching and consistent mentoring make every moment a teaching opportunity. The soft skills, when truly defined, become a smart and powerful skillset. This causes cast members to be stretched and equips them to become more than they ever expected. Your cast members are the cornerstones in driving magical moments that take the experience to a memorable level, whereby the consumers are swept off their feet.

In most situations, we completely underestimate this magical experience that becomes the key business driver. It is so important to create magical moments because the consumer gladly returns, which results in a repeat visit, eager to see if your team can maintain the standards, to show their friends.

You have to be constantly stage-ready, look impeccable, and have the show start on time. Ask yourself to look through the eyes of the consumer. One of the biggest crimes is being just average. By being average, there is no event, no real impression of exceeding expectations or motivating the consumer to return. Ask yourself, would you, under this circumstance, do business with yourself? As a visionary leader, you need to capture the essence of delivering a ceaseless commitment, evoking real-life magic by capturing the moment(s), by shifting one's mental emotion to that of excellence, and by delivering a quality-plus customer service experience. It begins with the positive energy and willingness of every cast member to buy-in to the commitment of excellence and thereby capturing these moments of magic. Excellence wins the moment and the day.

This will take a concerted effort by everyone to work at, to re-focus, reshape, and deliver a customer experience that captures how everyone really wants to be treated. Take care of those who will come back time and time again and who will be willing to share their wallets.

If Disney can build a 'kingdom,' I am convinced that many, many others can emulate the same strategic elements. This can be done by adopting these magical principles, by delivering impactful word scripts and tracks, by practicing these messages and rehearsing them, and by application of mental fortitude. Your cast members must be well-trained and knowledgeable. Pair up the newly hired members with the best ones on your team so they can learn effectively and see how it is done right. These kinds of advancements are possible when the complete organization buys-in.

"It is kind of fun to do the impossible. Whatever you do, do it well."

–Walt Disney

That is the secret of Disney's success, and I want you to promote it to become your signature. How does Disney do it? The secret is following the formula for $uccess!

The difference between winning and losing is often found in one thing: not quitting! The amazing secret to an exceptional, over-the-top, memorable customer service experience is in following the architect's blueprint and sticking to the principles to become more creative; it is in the willingness to do better. Your level of competition will result in birthing something very special. It is also about employee engagement and practice.

Employee engagement is about catching this vision, so it inspires one to create sustainable culture by looking and working on the positive details. Failure often takes place when principles are ignored or undermanaged. That is why the accountability of managers is so important; they have to be the encouragers and cheerleaders that help breathe life into those individuals so they can capture their personalized dreams. To deliver excellence, the process requires outstanding leadership, which will impact the entire cast, creating positive re-enforcement that enhances sustainability. Positive energy is like oxygen to one's soul; it brings out passionate ideas that are well-articulated. It is the management's responsibility to personally engage with the cast members and encourage them while guiding them in the right direction to elevate their career paths.

Customers love the attention to detail, words that are spoken, the environment, and the Disney-like magic that tops it off. The secret formula is a product of resilience and hard work, while failure comes when you lose the stick-to-it-iveness because you give in. So, roll up your sleeves and get the work done. You should have that inner burning desire to champion the cause in pursuit of excellence. This takes a lot of work with positive energy and focuses on creating a signature achievement.

Another secret to $uccess is to be competitive in every aspect of the business. Today's service managers have to focus on every aspect of the business, from the front end to the back shops, along with every tiny detail in between. This has to be done all the while coaching, mentoring, motivating their cast members, and holding them accountable for their actions. Today, businesses are much more complicated and definitely more difficult to understand and manage. A visionary leader must have a solid track record as well as a strong work ethic. He/she should make time to further invest in their valuable cast members who have an impeccable set of soft skills to educate consumers effectively about the amazing benefits and incredible value.

In many cases, consumers buy-in because they are motivated to buy value, which is what they seek. Remember, retention leads to loyalty, thus repeat business. Technicians in the back should have the necessary training to stay ahead and feel comfortable in handling these challenging high-tech vehicles. With a strong team, success and opportunities are unlimited. When everyone works for the same goals and objectives, it becomes an amazing ride.

You need to have clear communication and direction that is concise and precise. Do service advisors anticipate problems in advance? Have they learned from their past mistakes? Have they created a checklist of different scenarios and addressed how to avoid certain pain points while creating a solution model. The secret is to anticipate problems in advance. Listening is a critical skill; make sure you quickly note the consumer's concerns and issues and then repeat them back to the consumer. Always encourage the cast members to level up their game; high-performing teams have to work hard since this approach is the lifeblood of success.

As service consultants, stay focused and demonstrate a positive demeanor. Assure the consumer that once the diagnoses are complete and the digital vehicle inspection is completed, you will call and text them with updated information. Print out the manufacturer's maintenance service schedule based on the current mileage and review declined service, and know the service history. Provide a business card to the consumer with your name. Always acknowledge the waiting customers. Too often, we ignore the customer: no greeting, no eye contact, which makes them feel unwelcomed.

Another killer is when cast members are talking to each other about a customer, especially when customers are present or within hearing range. Today, staffers stay connected with their peers at all times, texting, googling, etc. I suggest this needs to be done during breaks. During work, this is unacceptable. Instead, you should be checking the vehicle status of your customers. As a team, you have shared accountability and ownership with a can-do attitude that you can perform at levels beyond customer expectations. To achieve above-average results, teamwork and engagement have to be impeccable. During the status call to the customer, another secret is sharing the amazing benefits and the incredible value. When it comes to addressing preventative maintenance based on the handling of the manufacturer's schedule, explain to them that it extends the service time and that the performance will be better and reduce the cost in the long term.

This is best achieved by using the term 'recommended maintenance' and using the word sharing versus telling, as it results in easier buy-ins. Another secret is constantly working on refining your process by expanding the scope. Put the confidence back into sales. Read and constantly review the benefits and value of all the preventative maintenance processes. Improve your game, step up, and become a superstar by putting in the work, as it will elevate your career path.

The impact of an over-the-top customer service is powerful regardless of what is happening in the economy. This outstanding customer experience acts as a firewall, which allows one to thrive, even during pandemics, and is built by delivering not just once but every time; the big 'C,' i.e., consistency. The service experience should be consistent and predictable. This is a direct reflection of building a 'trust economy.' With every consumer who comes in, make them feel appreciated, like a guest, and treat them as a VIP (very important person) since they are willingly sharing their wallets with you.

When consumers constantly receive the magic of the moment through sincerity in their gestures, their voice, and the tone they choose to use, You will instantly know that you are connecting with them. Elevate your level of communication. Use more selective language, focus on their needs, and listen to what they are saying; the failure to be an effective listener will lead to unhappy situations. Be more selective of the language to create a magical moment that makes the customer smile and feel much appreciated. This type of experience is like a drug, as the consumers would love availing your services, strictly because you helped in removing the pain points they experienced elsewhere.

The entire cast must clearly understand the process because each cast member has to invest in building a relationship that is personalized, professional, and relevant, like remembering their name and making a statement. Here is an example:

"Good to see you, Mrs. Brown."

"I am here to make your day as pleasant as possible. I have your order here and just want to review the concerns you are experiencing. Is there any other service that you need (pause)? I have checked your history, and it appears as a reminder, that you will need oil and lube on your next visit. While your vehicle is in the shop, we can add that to your service order (pause and look at her for her response, and add it with her authorization). While the staff diagnoses your concerns and since your car is already in the service bay, we would like to offer a Digital Vehicle Inspection as well as quick alignment with our latest Hunter Engineer Quick Check to make sure you are achieving maximum tire life and better fuel economy. I see that you have requested a courtesy ride to the office. I have held up the shuttle vehicle to make sure you get to your office on time. Lastly, what is your wish when we call to update you on the findings related to your engine light that the computer has detected? The cost is 'X' dollars is for the diagnosis, time, and charge. I just need your signature here. Have a good morning, Mrs. Brown, and I will be in touch as soon as our expertly trained techs diagnose the problem, and I will share the results with you."

The service consultant must constantly build a relationship that is personalized, professional, relevant, authentic, and transparent. It is also important that the service be delivered seamlessly. When the status call is made, the cast members must share the diagnoses, explain the how and why, and then use the education approach with the guest (consumer) while walking them through the repairs that are required, as well as sharing the DVI report. When they are well-informed, they see and sell themselves for any additional findings.

I have worked in the industry at all levels, and I often see the advisors rattle off the findings and the associate price without creating an ounce of value. In many cases, the consumer will respond by saying, *"Let me think about it."* With that statement not addressed, you are basically sending them down the road into the open arms of your competitors.

The last secret is you have to ask for the business/order. This is the test as to whether or not you have delivered. Knock, and the sale will be opened to you. The unforgivable sin, in too many cases, is we blurt out the price and not value. Value motivates consumers to say the little word, *"Yes."* These words will reward you many, many times, over and over again. To really pull all the stops, everyone has to practice these soft skills and implement them until they become good habits. Business is hard when old approaches persist within new realities. Today, many shops are stagnant primarily because they are not changing with the world that is. During my career and certainly in my role as a consultant, I witnessed that there comes a time when a service center becomes stale and stagnant. Everyone needs a push to bring in new energy, new ideas, new approaches to best practice, new proven processes, more effective strategies, and new insights to release successful tools that will produce effective results.

When it comes to pushing the bar of customer service experience higher, we have to look at the impeccable model by visiting a Disney theme park and examining all the intrinsic elements that make it the 'happiest place on Earth.' So why are you not doing more to build and further shape your kingdom? If you decide, you can build a magical kingdom; it is within your grasp. You should be laying the foundational bricks in building your own kingdom inside the walls of your service department.

So, let us start by looking around at the appearance of the outside of your building; does it look crisp, clean, and well-maintained? Has someone picked up the pieces of paper that blew around overnight? Now, stepping inside the building, does the waiting room look impeccable, clean, with comfortable seats, with social distancing in place? Are there a couple of daily newspapers, is the TV on a local news channel, is there a warm pot of coffee on, and are there a variety of magazines? What is the first impression you have when you look through the window into the service center? Do the floors and techs' workbenches appear to be clean? Is the overall image conducive to the consumer's liking?

Let us look at the cast members. Do they look like they were at a super bowl party all night long? What does the staff look like? Is their hair neatly cut? Are their beards trimmed? Is their smile welcoming? Are their uniforms clean? About the upfront cast members, do they appear ready, and does the surrounding stage reflect the image? Are the posters or electronic reader screen(s) up and functioning? It will tell who you are. Are all the key responses polished? Are the greetings the same? Is someone around to answer the telephone? In too many places, the cast member answers the phone and then immediately puts them on hold and, often, forgets about that guest!

Wow, that is a great way to lose a great guest. If that happens, take the telephone and call back as soon as possible. Ask yourself, did I do my very best? Are we, as a team, delivering a 'world-class customer service experience?' Everything needs to be taken into consideration in order to deliver a seamless customer service experience and for your customers to leave the service center more than satisfied.

The Takeaway

I believe that in order to be successful in the demanding automotive service business, you need to make your cast members the number one priority. Have them clearly understand that the customers are very demanding and expect a high-quality customer service experience and great workmanship. Thus, they have to completely kill the ugly churn monster by kicking it to the curb.

The upfront cast members have an even more demanding performance; they have to have strong knowledge of the industry, with excellent and effective communication and soft skills that bring a personal touch whereby they explain the verified problem, and then empower the consumer by educating them on the benefits and incredible value, or the 'what is in it for me.' The front-line cast member must execute a "Disney-like" experience in the process to keep the consumer informed and happy, just like Mickey Mouse, everyone's favorite character, who leads the 3 o'clock parade down Main street in Disney land. Like great actors, the front-line cast members must make the experience memorable by acting out the right lines, the best practices, and a solid and proven process.

Acknowledgement: *Material used in Chapter 3 (Becoming Irresistable) that was obtained from the article titled 'Becoming Irresistable: A New Model for Employee Engagement' published on Deloitte US website, has been used with permission. A permission letter stating their consent has been attached and can be found in the appendix section of the book.*

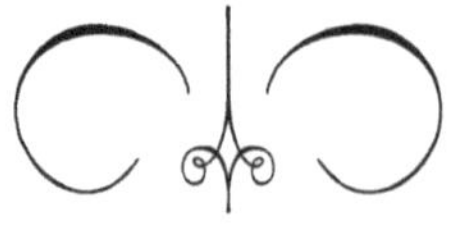

CHAPTER 3

BECOMING IRRESISTIBLE

A New Model for Employee Engagement

"Whatever we accomplish belongs to the entire group, a tribute to our combined effort."

-Walt Disney

Re-investing - Making Our Cast Members Our #1 Priority

We must breed a new culture by making cast members our number one priority. Have a weekly meeting, even just a quick one with all your team members. Constantly request input from the cast members because some brilliant ideas are like jewels and treasure.

If you want a higher quality of performance, have all cast members go the extra mile, i.e., no cutting corners, road test every vehicle to confirm that the diagnoses are spot on, the issues have been eliminated, and touch up the greasy fingerprints. Build up your service team, encourage them, ask how the family is doing, the kids, build good relationships, so the cast members feel like a valuable part of the team; treat them with the golden rule. In the past, during my consultant times, service managers too often berated the cast members, which led to resentment; this is not acceptable in any case. Turnover with staff is a costly ticket. Service managers should celebrate success, buy breakfast for them, give your team members time for doctor's appointments, allow them to leave early from time to time.

Also, share the re-focused items to provide a quality experience, new protocols, inform them that you have done a competitive market analysis in your direct market area, then discuss with the owner about an opportunity to increase the door rate and share a portion with the team members. This is a brilliant idea that really allows one to enhance the bottom line while sharing with staff as well.

Whatever you do, the entire team needs to embrace it because the more effort you make to win the hearts of the consumer, the more you would benefit. Everyone needs to be built up; it is like oxygen to the soul. I realized early on in my career, as I continued to grow that I had to be a more effective communicator. I also started a culture of zoom meetings to stay updated since consumers always want their vehicles returned ahead of schedule. I learned always to be sincere and generously praise and thank the cast members for delivering quality plus services that consumers love. Another key factor when dealing with more complicated repair scenarios is having the tech directly involve consumers as they move forward. Better yet, invest in AutoServe1 and see consumers buy-in at a higher rate. Smart devices work like magic as they switch the mindset of consumers from "No" to "Yes" as they see that they are safe and meet the industry standards.

Hunter Engineering, with their brilliant intelligence, is not a cost, rather an investment. It is all about the consumers; most of them will say “Yes” when the powerful document from the Hunter Engineering system is handed over to them. They have a ‘Wow!’ experience as they receive an opinion from a neutral third party which brings assurance and comfort.

The win is so big you cannot afford not to stay ahead of your competition. The machine is designed for the customers, so the buy-in is without a grudge or an over-eager staffer. However, put the brakes on first, let them sell themselves; That is why this smart tool is so important for your tool kit. They do the work that cast members may not be able to do as effectively. I was in a store as a consultant; we arranged for Hunter Engineering to install a demo machine. The first day, we had consumers buying 12 of the first 14 quick alignment checks, plus a good chunk of additional pieces like tie rods and ball joints which had an excessive play, etc. It was like Christmas. I love these systems because I know the impact they have on the consumer and, ultimately, the business.

Employees want to feel part of the process and know how the team, in general, is performing against the other stores within the chain or group. Let the staffers know how well they are doing, thus motivating the technicians to not sacrifice “quality” over “time.” Doing it right the first time is ultra-important. I prefer to share the results of our growth.

I believe employee engagement and alignment is the key to success; when we take the time to share the inspection results with the consumer, everyone wins. Sharing with cast members about how to take care of consumers while delivering a Disney-like experience makes these cast members feel they are in a partnership, which brings about great success. Cast members like to be informed about where the company is and where the true potential and opportunities are. High employee engagement equals high employee satisfaction and retention. A workplace should have an environment where cast members enjoy coming to work and leave fulfilled and excited about the opportunities for the next day. Research by Deloitte suggests that the issues of "retention and engagement" have risen to the top in the minds of business leaders, second only to the challenge of building global leadership. More than 70% of millennials expect their employers to focus on societal or mission-driven problems; 70% want to be creative at work and enjoy the satisfaction that comes with encouragement from the management and their support.

(From here forward to end of this chapter: used with permission by Deloitte US – Deloitte Review Issue 16 – January 27, 2015)

The employee-work contract has changed, compelling business leaders to build organizations that engage employees as sensitive, passionate, creative contributors. Two years of research and discussions with hundreds of clients suggest five major elements and underlying strategies that work together to make organizations "irresistible."

After decades of corporate discourse about the war for talent, it appears that the battle is over, and talent has won. Employees today have increased bargaining power, the job market is highly transparent, and attracting top-skilled workers is a highly competitive activity. Companies are now investing in analytical tools to figure out why people leave, and the topics of purpose, engagement, and culture weigh on the minds of business leaders everywhere. Our research suggests that the issues of "retention and engagement" have risen to No. 2 in the minds of business leaders, second only to the challenge of building global leadership.[1] These concerns are grounded in disconcerting data:

- Gallup's 2014 research shows that only 13% of all employees are "highly engaged," and 26% are "actively disengaged."[2]
- Glassdoor, a company that allows employees to rate their employers, reports that only 54% of employees recommend their company as a place to work.[3]
- In the high-technology industry, two-thirds of all workers believe they could find a better job in less than 60 days if they only took the time to look.[4]
- 80% of organizations believe their employees are overwhelmed with information and activity at work (21 % cite the issue as urgent), yet fewer than 8 % have programs to deal with the issue.[5]
- More than 70 % of Millennials expect their employers to focus on societal or mission-driven problems; 70 % want to be creative at work, and more than two-thirds believe it is management's job to provide them with accelerated development opportunities in order for them to stay.[6]

The employee-work contract has changed: People are operating more like free agents, more so than in the past. In short, the balance of power has shifted from employer to employee, forcing business leaders to learn how to build an organization that engages employees as sensitive, passionate, creative contributors. We call this a shift from improving employee engagement to a focus on building an irresistible organization.

Time For a Change

One of the issues we must address is the aging idea of an employee engagement survey. While such measures of engagement have been used for years, organizations tell us they are not providing modern, actionable solutions. Consider the typical process: Companies deploy annual surveys to benchmark a company's level of employee satisfaction from year to year. Most use vendor-provided surveys that claim to be statistically validated ways of measuring engagement. The marketplace of survey providers, which is around $1 billion in size, is largely staffed by industrial psychologists who have built statistical models that correlate turnover with various employment variables. The pioneer in this market, Gallup, promotes a survey of 12 simple factors that statistically predict retention.[7] Other vendors have their own models. Many focus on the characteristics of leadership, management, career opportunities, and other elements of the work environment.

While none of these models are "wrong," companies tell us the surveys do not prescribe actionable results. In a recent survey among 80 of the most advanced users of engagement surveys, only half believe their executives know how to build a culture of engagement.[8] Among the broader population, the percentage is far lower.

Consider the radical changes that have taken place at work: Employees operate in a transparent job market where in-demand staff finds new positions in their inboxes. Organizations are flattened, giving people less time with their direct managers.[9] Younger employees have increased the demand for rapid job rotation, accelerated leadership, and continuous feedback. Finally, the work environment is highly complex — where we once worked with a team in an office, we now work 24/7 with email, instant messages, conference calls, and mobile devices that have eliminated the barriers between our work and personal lives.

These changes to the workplace have altered the engagement equation, forcing us to rethink it. For example, a well-known pharmaceutical company found that its executives and scientists in China were leaving the company at an alarming rate. The annual engagement survey provided no such information to help diagnose this problem. By running a statistical analysis on all the variables among these departing high-potential workers, the company realized that in China, unlike other parts of the world, people were expecting very high rates of compensation increase every year.

The job market there was highly competitive, so people were being poached based on salary progression alone. Today, more and more companies are deploying analytical solutions to predict retention, correlating factors such as compensation, travel schedule, manager, and demographics to understand why certain people are less engaged than others.[10] But the answers are hard to find. High-technology companies, for example, throw benefits at employees to see which ones stick—unlimited vacation, free food, health clubs, parties, stock options, and fun offices are common. Do these all result in high engagement? Most companies cannot really tell you.

So, what matters today? How can we create an organization in today's work environment that is magnetic and attractive, creates a high level of performance and passion, and continuously monitors problems that need to be fixed?

Make Work Irresistible

Our research suggests that we need to rethink the problem. There are three issues to address:

1. Companies need to expand their thinking about what "engagement" means today, giving managers and leaders specific practices they can adopt and holding line leaders accountable. Here we suggest 5 elements and 20 specific practices.

2. Companies need tools and methods that measure and capture employee feedback and sentiment on a real-time, local basis so they can continuously adjust management practices and the work environment at a local level. These tools include employee feedback systems as well as data analytics systems that help identify and predict factors that create low engagement and retention problems.

3. Leaders in business and HR need to raise employee engagement from an HR program to a core business strategy.

A Refreshed Model for Engagement

After two years of research and discussions with hundreds of clients, we uncovered five major elements (and 20 underlying strategies) that work together to make organizations "irresistible."

These 20 factors fit together into a whole system of engagement in an organization (figure 1), one that is held together through culture.

A Note About Compensation and Benefits

Most studies show that compensation is an important factor in employee satisfaction. Research by Aon Hewitt, for example, shows that it ranks among the top five drivers (but is not number one).[11] In this article, we do not discuss compensation because much research shows that pay is a "hygiene factor," not an "engagement factor." In other words, in most cases, if compensation is not high enough, people will leave — but increasing compensation does not directly increase engagement (with certain exceptions). One organization we studied told us that among the highest-potential employees, the organization could directly correlate pay increases with retention — but among the remaining 90% of the workforce, compensation simply had to be competitive and fair within job families. Our discussions with clients confirmed that once their pay is competitive and fair, the 20 issues we have discussed in this paper have a much greater effect.

1. Make Work Meaningful

The first and perhaps most important part of employee engagement is job-person fit. We need to make sure jobs are meaningful, people have the tools and autonomy to succeed, and that we select the right people for the right job. This is anything but a simple undertaking.

Nearly every job has been changed and often transformed by technology, and we constantly look for ways to do more with less. Well-run companies constantly look at the work they do, trying to find ways to outsource more to technology and produce more output with less expensive human input. Despite these pressures to improve productivity, research shows that when we enrich jobs, giving people more autonomy, decision-making power, time, and support, the company makes more money.[12] Psychologist Daniel Pink writes that people are driven by "autonomy, mastery, and purpose."[13] Individuals crave work that lets them leave a unique fingerprint on a finished product. Zeynep Ton, a Massachusetts Institute of Technology professor, in her book 'The Good Jobs Strategy,' shows that retailers like Whole Foods, Costco, UPS, and Mercadona deliver higher profitability per employee by giving their employees above-average wages and greater control over their jobs.[14] The idea of "lowering the cost of labor" to save money backfires because people simply become less productive as their workload goes up.

At Mercadona and Costco, for example, stores are staffed by people cross-trained to handle many positions: They manage cash registers, stock shelves, rearrange the store, develop promotions, and manage others. The result is a set of highly empowered teams that have the training and freedom to be both autonomous and productive as well as above-average retention and engagement rates. As we design jobs to be meaningful, we must also carefully *select the right person for each job*. Fewer than 40 % of all hiring teams use any form of formal prehire assessment: Most managers look for relevant experience, college credentials, or GPA.[15] While these seem to be sound criteria for success, when organizations study the characteristics of high performers, they find that other "fit factors" actually drive success and happiness on the job.[16] A movie theater company found, for example, that theater employees who drive the highest levels of customer satisfaction and concession sales are not those with good grades or strong academic experience but rather people who "like to have fun" and "love to serve others." An insurance company found that the best salespeople were not those from top schools but rather those who had experience in the auto industry and no typos on their resumes. When we hire people who fit, they perform well, and they love their work.[17]

The concept of culture has also become an important part of job fit. Zappos, a company that prides itself on culture as a strategy, uses its 10 core values to assess people for cultural fit in the early stages of the application process.[18] By getting to know candidates well (through online and phone meetings) before people even apply for jobs, Zappos can assess fit and help people decide if they should even apply for a job. This type of assessment has helped Zappos maintain a high level of engagement, low turnover, and its place among one of the best customer service providers in online retail.[19] Research also shows that meaningful work takes place in small teams. Jeff Bezos, the CEO of Amazon.com, is reported to have said, "If there are more than two pizzas in the room for lunch, then the team is too big." Small teams feel empowered, they make decisions faster, and members get to know each other and feel more willing to lend a hand.[20]

Finally, engaged people need *time to think, create, and rest.* At Google, the policy is called "20 % time", a day a week set aside to work on something new or outside your normal job function. A well-known retailer, for example, sends workers home when the store is slow. They are free to run errands, have lunch with their families, or just relax. Then, when things get busy, they return to the store. This company is one of the most profitable in its industry, in part because slack time gives its workforce the freedom to take care of their home lives and put more effort into their work.

It may seem counterproductive to let people take time off during the week, but the opposite is true. Overworked people tend to burn out, produce lower-quality output, provide lower levels of customer service, become depressed, and sometimes just flail around in their exhaustion.[21] Giving people time lets them relax, engage, and perform better.

2. Foster Great Management

The second element of an irresistible organization is the one business and HR leaders think about the most: management. I use the word "management" here, not leadership, to refer to the daily, weekly, and monthly activities managers use to guide, support, and align their people.

In many ways, management is the most important capability we have. CEOs can create strategies, investors can optimize capital, and marketers can create demand, but when it comes to building products and offerings, serving clients, and developing internal processes, middle managers make things happen.

We each thrive on our ability to contribute to the greater good. Management's job is to set goals, support people, coach for high performance, and provide feedback to continuously improve. Investment in fundamental management practices has a tremendous impact on engagement, performance, and retention.[22] In many ways, management is the most important capability we have. CEOs can create strategies, investors can optimize capital, and marketers can create demand. Still, when it comes to building products and offerings, serving clients, and developing internal processes, middle managers make things happen. In our review of engagement issues, the first area we found is the importance of simple, clear goals. When people have clearly defined goals that are written down and shared freely, everyone feels more comfortable, and more work gets done. Goals create alignment, clarity, and job satisfaction — and they have to be revisited and discussed regularly.

Goal setting is a challenge. Only 5 % of companies even attempt to develop aligned goals, and, among these, only 6 % regularly revisit them.[23] Too many companies write down annual goals and only look at them at the end of the year. We found that companies that revisit goals quarterly have threefold greater improvement in performance and retention than those that revisit goals yearly.[24]

High-performing managers create simple goals, make sure they are clear and transparent, and revisit them regularly. Google, for example, uses an agile goal-setting process called OKR (objectives and key results), which was originally developed at Intel.[25] The process is simple and effective: Each individual (from CEO down) sets ambitious and measurable objectives (like "launch Gmail version X by year-end") and is asked to define "key results" that monitor their progress. Everyone's OKRs are public, so it is easy to see what the CEO or your peer is holding himself or herself accountable for. At Google, this creates alignment because employees can see who is dependent on their work.[26] People feel comfortable that they know what to do, they see what others are working on, and the measurement of their performance is clear.

The second management practice that drives engagement is coaching. A coaching culture is a practice That is most highly correlated with business performance, employee engagement, and overall retention.[27] When new managers are promoted to supervisory positions, they often think their job is to direct or evaluate people. While directed management is important, it plays a smaller role than one might think. It is the coaching and development role of management that is the most valuable.[28]

What makes a great coach? As Marcus Buckingham describes the role, great coaches understand people's strengths, move them into positions and rearrange work to leverage these strengths, and coach them to build on these strengths. 29 Nothing makes a person feel better about work than being able to be highly successful. The third factor in "irresistible" management is *leadership development*. Organizations with high levels of employee engagement focus on developing great leaders. They invest heavily in management development and ensure that new leaders are given ample support.

High-impact leadership organizations spend 1.5–3 times more on management development than their peers.[30] This continuous focus on building leaders, connecting leaders, and giving leaders the coaching they need is critical to building a highly engaged workforce.

The fourth issue is the need to simplify or reengineer the annual *performance appraisal*. This process, which has been institutionalized in more than 75 % of all the companies we visit, is among the most damaging and disheartening processes employees face each year. Only 8 % of surveyed companies think the process is worth the time they put into it. The focus on rating and ranking takes the focus away from the coaching and development that people often desperately need.[31]

In many companies, the process does not involve enough continuous feedback, places too much weight on the actual rating, and often does not encourage hyper-performers to perform at an even higher level. The concept of "forced ranking," popularized in the 1960s, is now falling away because it strips the autonomy and judgment of leaders, often discourages very high performers, and rewards those in the middle.[32]

Finally, companies need to remember that management's job is not to manage work but rather to develop, coach, and help people. Rewarding managers only for making their numbers incentivizes what we call "talent hoarding": attracting the best people and holding onto them for years. To help people get the coaching and support they need to grow, forward-thinking companies reward managers for what we call "talent production": developing people who leave their teams. This continuous development is a management culture widely used in high-engagement companies.

3. Establish a Flexible, Humane, Inclusive Workplace

The third major element of an irresistible organization is the need to build a flexible, humane, and inclusive workplace.

Most employees today have complicated lives. Studies show that 68 % of women would rather have more free time than make more money, and while 40 % of professional men work more than 50 hours per week, 80 % would like to work fewer hours.[33] Given the nature of work today, if leaders want people to engage with their organizations, they have to give them a *flexible and supportive work environment*. SAS, the No. 2 place to work for the last 15 years, has an in-house daycare center, gym, and pool, and the company's turnover rate is below 2 %.[34] Similarly, Google has a bowling alley and yoga rooms. Free food, yoga classes, happy hours, commute buses with Internet access, and even free laundry service have now become commonplace in high-pressure companies across a wide range of industries. These are no longer just "perks"; they are essential elements of making work fit into our lives.

In addition to such benefits and employee wellness programs, research also shows that open, flexible workplaces have a major impact on engagement. They bring executives out into the open (Mayor Bloomberg created an open workspace in New York City, which was credited with bringing teams together to rapidly respond to city crises); they enable people to meet more easily (The new circular Apple campus is designed to encourage groups to meet others); and they give people highly flexible places to work, depending on the way they feel on a given day (Zappos lets employees work from local restaurants, where the company pays for Wi-Fi). Research shows that introverts still want a quiet office, but modern workspaces give people the flexibility to be together or alone, depending on the task at hand.[35]

A second key engagement driver is the need for continuous and ongoing recognition. As soft as it seems, saying "thank you" is an extraordinary tool for building an engaged team. We studied this topic and found that "high-recognition companies" have 31% lower voluntary turnover than companies with poor recognition cultures.[36]

These companies build a culture of recognition through social reward systems (tools that give people points or kudos to reward others), weekly or monthly thank-you activities, and a general culture of appreciating everyone from top to bottom. The key to success here is to create a social environment where recognition can flow from peer to peer, freeing managers from being the judge and jury of employee recognition.

Companies that build this culture see a tremendous impact. When JetBlue implemented a peer-to-peer recognition system focused on company values, employee satisfaction surged by 88 %.[37] And there are physiological effects as well: Researchers have proven that when you thank someone, it releases oxytocin, a hormone that makes people more relaxed, collaborative, and happy.[38] Finally, highly engaged workplaces are also inclusive and diverse: People feel comfortable being themselves. While 71 % of organizations try to foster diversity and inclusion, only 11 % have such an environment today. 39 Even worse, only 23 % hold their CEOs accountable for building a diverse and inclusive environment; instead, leadership often delegates this work to a director within HR.[40] Press about the lack of diversity in Silicon Valley has highlighted how this issue plagues some of the fastest-growing companies in the world.[41]

Diversity and inclusion is not an HR strategy; it is a business strategy. Not only do diverse workplaces attract people from a wider sample, but research also shows that teams that operate in an inclusive culture outperform their peers by a staggering 80 %.[42] In a recent study of high-turnover companies conducted by Quantum Workplace, the second-highest-rated issue in employee engagement was the organization's unwillingness to "listen to an employee's perspectives."[43] While this is a fairly broad statement, it speaks to the issue of inclusion at an organizational level. How do organizations become more inclusive? Inclusion usually comes from the top: Leaders must overcome their unconscious biases and make every effort to listen, create open forums for discussion, and promote people with varied backgrounds (gender, nationality, race, age) who embrace listening and inclusive values. Our research shows that inclusion, unlike diversity, is a cultural issue — one that requires support from top-level leaders as well as all levels of management.

4. Create Ample Opportunities for Growth

When top performers leave a company, the most popular comment they make is, "I just didn't see the right opportunities here."

Let us face it: We often go to work with selfish interests. If we do not feel we are going to progress in our chosen role or career, we are likely to look elsewhere. Most engagement research shows that learning opportunities, professional development, and career progression are among the top drivers of employee satisfaction. Employees under the age of 25 rates professional development as their number one driver of engagement, and this is the number two priority for workers up to age 35.[44] As employees get older, their focus on development shifts away from mobility and upward progression in favor of aligning a job with long-term career goals. Building opportunities for growth is a complex and systemic challenge. First, there must be developmental opportunities, both formal and informal, that let people learn on the job, take developmental assignments, and find support when they need help. This means designing onboarding and transition management programs, developing a culture of support and learning, and giving people time to learn.

Second, a company must support and honor what we call *facilitated talent mobility*. Most people will not be promoted every year or two (although high-potential Millennials often expect it), but they want to feel that they are growing and can take on new assignments in their chosen area. Managers, and the company as a whole, need to support and facilitate internal mobility, giving people the freedom to try something new and move from a role where they are highly productive to one where they may be a trainee again.

Finally, organizations must look at their management and leadership behaviors to make sure that learning, development, and mobility are rewarded. Most leaders are rewarded for "making their numbers." While this is certainly important, leaders must also be rewarded for developing people, moving people into the best roles, and keeping retention high. Organizations with a strong learning culture are 92 % more likely to develop novel products and processes, 52 % more productive, 56 % more likely to be the first to market with their products and services, and 17 % more profitable than their peers.[45] Their engagement and retention rates are also 30–50 % higher.

One of the best examples of a learning culture is what happens in a retail environment. Most customers have been in stores where employees are trained and empowered. As soon as something is missing or perhaps hard to find, the employee figures out where it is, finds the right size, and helps customers complete a purchase.

Unempowered employees who are not cross-trained, however, may just tell customers to ask someone else. A major home improvement retailer studied store-by-store performance and found that teams that cross-train their sales leaders regularly are generating 10–15 % higher revenue and as much as 20 % higher engagement scores.

Remember, an irresistible organization is one that employees would never want to leave. What better way to create such a place than to give people lots of opportunities to grow and advance?

5. Establish Vision, Purpose, and Transparency in Leadership

The final and perhaps most important element in the irresistible organization is leadership. Our research suggests that four leadership practices most directly impact employee engagement.

The first is to develop and communicate a strong sense of purpose. When organizations define their success through the eyes of their customers, stakeholders, or society, people come alive.[46] Our research shows that "mission-driven" companies have 30 % higher levels of innovation and 40 % higher levels of retention, and they tend to be first or second in their market segment.

How do you create purpose, mission, and soul? As John Mackey suggests, define your company's value in terms of all its stakeholders: employees, investors, partners, and customers.[47] When all stakeholders benefit, the business performs well. Pharmaceutical companies are redefining themselves as wellness companies; retailers are redefining themselves as places for healthy food; tech companies define themselves as businesses to help people obtain information, and the list goes on. When you offer people a mission and purpose greater than financial return, you attract passionate individuals who want to contribute. And that brings a level of commitment and engagement no compensation package can create. During the heat of the space race, a group of reporters visited NASA (a mission-driven organization) and saw a janitor walking toward them with a broom in hand.

As part of their story-telling, they took out their cameras and asked the janitor, "So what is your job at NASA?" The janitor looked into the camera and said straight on, "It is my job to help put a man on the moon."[48] How many of your employees can answer a question like this? Remember, an irresistible organization is one that employees would never want to leave. What better way to create such a place than to give people lots of opportunities to grow and advance?

The second important element in leadership today is *transparency*. Thanks to social networks and the Internet, we are all accustomed to rapid, open, transparent communications. If your company is having a bad quarter, has committed fraud, has caused an accident was sued, or is possibly penalized for a compliance violation, tell your people as promptly as possible. Likewise, when you have a good quarter, someone achieves a particularly notable success, or a customer tells you something wonderful, share this as well. Whole Foods goes so far as to release every employee's total salary and bonuses from the previous year in its annual wage disclosure report. If employees are concerned about their compensation, they are encouraged to make an appointment with HR to discuss their issues.[49] Transparency is particularly difficult for traditional leaders.

They often believe they can "manage the truth" through PR, communications specialists, or timed release of information. Today, this typically fails, and people immediately see the deception. New research shows that among Millennials, transparency from leadership rates is among the most important drivers of company loyalty.[50]

Third, leaders must continuously invest in people. High-engagement companies have executives who spend money on learning, regularly meet with teams and provide feedback, and genuinely care about each individual. Our research on "high-impact learning organizations," conducted in 2005, 2008, and 2011 (before, during, and after the last recession), showed each year that companies that "overinvest" in L&D (spending per employee) rated highest in employee retention, innovation, and customer service and outperformed their peers threefold in long-term profitability.[51] This trend shows that investment in people matters during good times and bad. Finally, our research suggests that senior leaders must continuously focus on inspiration. Through their words, communications, and actions, it is the top executives who ultimately engage everyone in the organization. By talking about the future, sharing the vision, and translating the business strategy into meaningful, personal concepts, leadership can be one of the most important drivers of engagement.

A Focus on Simplicity

As we illustrate at the bottom of the model, highly engaged companies work very hard to make work simple. They remove administrative overhead (compliance processes, formal check-off processes, multistep processes) in favor of trust, autonomy, and a focus on cooperation.

Simplicity, or the removal of formal bureaucratic overhead, can have a dramatic impact on work satisfaction. A series of work-productivity studies by the University of Rotterdam shows that workers who operate in highly complex environments tend to have increased levels of cardiovascular and other illnesses unless they are given extraordinary amounts of autonomy and local support. Without increased amounts of empowerment and local control, complexity can lead to high levels of error and stress.[52] Southwest Airlines, one of the top 20 rated employers in 2014, has honed simplicity and empowerment in its business model.[53] The company focuses heavily on employee empowerment in its management training, letting the local team (the airplane crew) make all the decisions they need to run safely, on time, and budget.[54] The company also works hard to keep its entire business simple: Southwest uses a single airplane model (Boeing ۷۳۷) and common boarding and reservation processes for every flight. The company has celebrated more than 40 years of profitability and continues to score among the highest in customer satisfaction year after year.

Capturing Real-time Feedback

How do organizations implement these 20 practices in an integrated and holistic way? Our advice falls into two categories.

First, HR and leadership must develop a complete understanding and mindset of these factors and how they all are interrelated. Almost every management practice impacts employee engagement, so while we focus on performance, growth, and innovation, we must simultaneously focus on the impact each strategy has on individual people.

Second, it is important to instrument your company to obtain regular, unbiased, and anonymous feedback. People always want to talk about what is working and what is not in their company. An annual employee survey is far too slow and limiting. Today, pulse survey tools, sentiment monitoring tools, and employee sensing tools give employees various ways to express their feelings and provide direct feedback to managers and peers. Four new tools — Culture Amp, BlackbookHR, TINYhr, and BetterCompany — each have different ways of actively measuring employee feedback and sentiment. Consider these tools as the anonymous "heartbeat monitors" of your business.

Putting Employee Engagement at the Center of Everything We Do

If we do not have teams committed to our mission, passionate about their work, and willing and ready to work together, we cannot possibly succeed over time.

While 90 % of executives understand the importance of employee engagement, fewer than 50 % understand how to address this issue.[55] Today's technology-flooded world of work has become complex, demanding, and integrated into our lives. Even though 79 % of companies today find it daunting and difficult, they can plot their path to the future and design organizations that will thrive with passion, performance, and engagement by focusing on the five elements of irresistible organizations.

Chapter 4

Projecting a Financial Business Model of Constant Double-digit Growth

"Of course, the key is to introduce the right offers to the right customers at the right times, not everything to everyone all the time."

–Gary DeSai

Virtually, many auto service centers feel they are doing a reasonably good job with customer service. It is important to keep in mind Shep Hyken's statement about delivering an average customer service experience: "Average is not pretty."

So, what is the best measuring stick for performance? From my five-decade experience in the auto service industry, I have realized beyond doubt that double-digit sales are driven by delivering all the little extras that make the customer service experience like that of visiting the happiest place on earth, often known as Disneyland.

If those of you in the auto service industry grasp this concept and apply this insight to roll out a passionate approach while empathizing and caring for the customer, if you can read their uncertainness, all the while assuring them that you have got it covered, it will become an awesome and magical service moment. Consumers will fall in love with this experience like that of going to Disneyland. Sure, at Disney Theme Park, guests pay a big ticket to experience the magical moments; however, we have to have that same mindset where we can build our own auto "kingdom." Become a dreamer and live the dream you have. If you do it right, it will be like that of winning the "power lottery."

Everyone in the team must commit to raising the "bar of par excellence." This is where the secret lies, over-delivering is a must, and all the rest will fall into place.

A service That is just functional is considered average. In other words, even though the work got done, no extra effort was made to make the event special, nothing That is too exciting; thus, the customer has no reason to return. As a leader, you have to pull the cast members together and lay out a new vision. Implement the strategies and ideas mentioned in this book, and introduce them one step at a time. With commitment from everyone in the team, miracles can surely happen. Only you, as a leader, can change the whole outlook of your auto service department, so choose the best possible practices and stick to them while holding everyone accountable. Be 100% committed while engaging and aligning 100% buy-ins by 100% of the team.

That is where the focus needs to be. I make the argument that your energy, positive body language, tone of voice, smile, and selection of words express the mood. Consumers will feel like they are getting the V.I.P. treatment, and they love it that you are fussing over them. The customer knows it when you make it a memorable event. There is a saying that, "The first and last impressions make an everlasting impression." An older friend used to tell me, *"Don, you need a checkup, from the neck up,"* Or he often used this one as well, *"Funk, think! it could be a brand-new experience."* I have taken this to heart!

The secret, right after delivering a jaw-dropping customer service experience, is **investing in artificial intelligence and smart devices;** Hunter Engineering and AutoServe1, respectively, totally and completely engage and align with the enhanced experience that customers require today. These are brilliant pieces of technology that, without question, allow auto service managers to present a different third-party analytic snapshot that brings great insight to the consumer. These documents impact the consumer immediately and change their mindset as they bring a completely new eye-opening insight that human services cannot quite deliver. It is revealing and powerful.

These two amazing companies are run-away corporations that are industry leaders and change the consumer's mind from silently thinking 'No' to pondering over the empirical evidence without a grudge and confirming that those items are a required repair or service. The results obtained from these smart tools change the landscape and drive sales in an upward trajectory that is shocking. These smart devices and AI tools are designed to help consumers grasp the reality within these brilliant documents.

The auxiliary benefits are stunning; you can go to their websites and read what the other operators, be they big or small, are saying. They are offering raving reviews of the added benefits. The pictures taken by the 8-mounted cameras capture and show the complete condition before the vehicle is handed over to the technicians. Upon the return of loaner vehicles, a quick check drive-through can easily capture and identify any dings and scratches, etc.It has saved dealers thousands of dollars.

In another scenario, the consumer has claimed that their vehicle was damaged during the service and repair processes. The pre-entry of the consumer's vehicle captures the actual status of the exterior condition before entering the service bay, which comes in handy in such situations. The benefit is huge. It protects your bottom-line profits to help hold your P&L statement in great shape, which otherwise in so many cases, becomes an added repair expense. As they say, this is a no-brainer. Now you see the bigger and brighter picture known as reality. Business with loaners is a cost, and avoiding additional costs is a big game-changer. The savings this smart tool provides help pay for the investment in a few months.

Even at the point of check out, it is a great opportunity to leave a lasting expression; here is an example:

"Thank you so much for allowing our team to take care of your auto services needs today. We greatly appreciate your patronage as a valued client. We are always here for you."

Yes, and then ask them to share their experience on various social media channels. The upside will attract a lot of new customers, which is a huge bonus!

That is exactly why I believe we have to roll out the red carpet and make it a special and memorable experience, whereby the consumer becomes the evangelist of your brand and is willing to share about your services on their personal social media platforms. The memorable experience allows your business to have exponential double-digit growth year after year. Amazing customer service experience is the number 1 driver for your business. I experienced this, and I lived this year after year. Your CSI (Customer Service Index) will go through the roof. You can never lose sight of this; That is why I strongly believe that making and investing in your cast members sets the tone. It is about encouraging them and growing with them into special-equipped team players. The real joy is when they come and share their feelings of thankfulness because you have impacted their lives and helped them build their careers. That is a rewarding piece!

It is difficult to measure the full impact. However, the double-digit plus growth of 20% and beyond is the real tell; the CSI numbers and the direct feedback are another big tell-tale factor. However, you have to earn and own every interaction 100% of the time, with 100% of the cast members, with 100% buy-in 100% of the time. Time passes very quickly; our window of opportunity closes faster than we realize. Hence, take time to maximize any opportunity you get.

If the organization wants to excel with constant and consistent double-digit performance, the leader and the cast members need to have the right skills; we become what we desire, and we must work toward having a solid career.

It is totally about the empowerment of educating one person (the consumer) who should be treated like a guest, in a clear, concise, and precise manner that helps them understand the value. Qualify the consumer by also asking if the maintenance has been recently done. Now That is the drill you have to put into your "smart and success toolbox." With preventive maintenance items, begin by saying that the technician is "recommending" based on the mileage and/or time. Sincerely helping customer after customer while fine-tuning those scripts or word tracks will ultimately result in cast members becoming superstars.

Let us factor in the approach of "How to educate consumers to see 'what is in it for me.'" Value is what motivates consumers. Share three points, be it an amazing benefit or an incredible value. Here is the message you have to deliver:

"Mrs. Jones, as the wheel alignment indicates, green is good, red is not good, (hand the consumer the printout). Doing the wheel alignment now will allow you to obtain the full life cycle of the tire according to the manufacturer's mileage projection, and since tires are expensive, doing the required wheel alignment adjustments will extend the life of the steering components almost indefinitely. These are expensive and require additional labor to install. Lastly, by having the vehicle rolling forward without the resistance, you can improve your fuel economy by up to 4 to 6 percentage points, and fuel is expensive as well, so you will be able to save here as well."

Consumers need to be empowered and educated rather than sold.

Here is another important piece of advice besides the education element. As a cast member, you cannot fake it. You need to have solid industry knowledge, as well as effective communication skills. Applying this insight requires a lot of training. The additional factors must play well; demonstrate correct body language, and show that you believe this, the tone of your voice should project confidence with a little emotional energy, and your posture should be upright, which indicates you are looking and performing to the best of your capability.

When it comes to doing preventative maintenance, like a wheel alignment, you have to nail the script in an upbeat, positive manner. Hunter Engineering does all the heavy lifting. This artificial piece of intelligence that Hunter Engineering has trotted out is amazing. Refer to the chapter 'Winning Big With Hunter Engineering'; it will knock the socks off you and the consumer. I have experienced and lived with the benefits of it. I want to make one thing abundantly clear: I'm not advocating for them, I'm advocating for **you and the clients of today** who are your real opportunity.

I go into an auto service center after having done a deep dive into the numbers and explain exactly what I want to uncover. In most cases, their boardrooms do not have any natural light (windows). I intentionally ask the owner to bring in lunch for all staff (cast members) and invite all the cast members to join a business meeting to hear me out.

During the meeting, I ask for input from the cast members, so it becomes more of a partnership, and these techs become more involved, and they know the benefits for technicians, and all other cast members, including the C.E.O. It is strictly about a new "Killer Business Plan," so I suggest making the best of everything and earning more from reaping the new opportunities (approaches) that have proven successful, and thus, are rewarding.

I search where the light switch is located, and turn it off, and ask them to focus on the words I am about to share. This amazing service industry has to share the benefits for the techs, for the business, and for the consumers by applying the best industry practices without ever cheating the consumer. Then, I pause for a moment and turn the lights back on. By doing this little exercise, these individuals refresh their internal computers, so they can see clearer, hear sharper, and see a greater impact which will change the mindset of technicians and owners, and other cast members, including front liners. As a service manager, it is part of their role and responsibility to invest and equip the team for much greater success, with a more positive outlook in terms of their careers and enhanced futures.

Then, I proceed with the meeting by saying that I have a question for everyone. The question is, who wants to earn more and become more and be more excited about their future? Their careers? I first have to peel the skin off their eyes so they see a whole new refreshing picture. The cast members across the board become excited about going forward. Turning the boardroom's lights back on allows them to witness firsthand the power and impact of the best practices and proven strategies.

I had taken on a thirteen-month assignment to manage an auto service center in Calgary as their existing service manager suffered a serious illness. The number 1 failure in the auto service field is in the wheel alignment sector. I realized the opportunity that wheel alignments would bring a dramatic boost in sales. More importantly, the consumer, by having the wheels aligned to fall within the manufacturer's spec, would extend tire life, etc. Since today's larger tires are more expensive, getting these necessary adjustments done would remove the stress and fatigue on steering components, such as tie rods, and lastly, increase the fuel economy. The benefits would be, first for the consumer, then the technician, and finally, the business.

The cost is concerning or almost alarming, and business owners are always interested in what would be a reasonable time frame for recovering the cost. How long would it take to pay off this smart AI tool? I indicated that having the Hunter Engineering Quick Alignment machine would pay for itself within two to three months or maybe a little longer considering the newest technology. If this is a concern, and it should be, call your Hunter Engineering specialist and talk to the sales representative, based on your annual traffic, they will map out the timeline.

This store I was consulting with was in the top quartile in a group/chain of approximately 500 stores, so I did a quick check on how many wheel alignments had been done over the past 12 months; the number was 489. With the insights I had gained from my experience, I felt very confident that the opportunity was great. During the next 13 months of my stay, we ordered the Hunter Quick Check machine, and after waiting to have it shipped and then have it installed and calibrated, we were off and running. The training was very straightforward and when implemented, (i.e., 100% wheel alignment checks on 100% of the vehicles by 100% of the cast members), generated a great return on investment. The turn-around time was three months. Not a bad investment, I must say.

The Impact of a Solid Killer Business Plan CSX

Here is the impact on the projected financial business model, using a conservative growth number of 15% in traffic (a key KPI-key performance indicator). Of the 261 working days, Monday to

Friday, footstep/customers would project up to 300 or more in your business.

The Revenue Growth Model of the AutoServe1 study of 600,000 invoices from 200 shops is certainly a great sample size. A "no inspection" plan generated an average invoice of $418.00. Every shop should deploy this smart tool, realizing it is not a cost but rather a generator of income that assures safer and better vehicle inspection. AS1 Digital Inspection process generates $93 more or a 22% increase. When the AS1 inspection report is sent to the customer via text, it provides a picture that is powerful and impacts the consumer in an even greater way so you can get a return on your investment. This evidence sways them to authorize doing the service of the findings because seeing is believing; thus, they act based on evidence. The impact of texting generates an additional 13% to bring the average invoice to $564, which is a 35% increase in growth. Wow! The discussion of cost is now certainly valid. It is NOT a cost, but rather a greater return on investment.

Example:

300 more customers multiplied by $564 = $169,200

Let us use 10 more customers per day.

10 customers more each day multiplied by $564 per customer = $5640

Eliminating Saturday and Sunday, thus using 261 days = $1,466,400

In the auto service business, Labor and Parts are a one-to-one split. This generates $733,200 (labor sales) at 30% margins = $220,860 of profit.

Add in parts, Total profit = $441,720

This would require you to hire one more technician who is efficient and productive. Just stop for a moment, and think: if you had one extra bay that was not being utilized, this definitely would have an impact. A 50-bay auto service center can generate one million dollars a month in labor: multiply that by twelve months, and this generates $12 million. Do the math with one-to-one parts and labor: now you have $24M at 30% profit. Deploying all these best practices and proven processes with solid strategies will produce stunning profits. Do the math and see for yourself.

The Takeaway

The goal of this chapter, "Projecting A Financial Business Model of Constant Double-Digit Growth," is to enhance the various delivery points. Today, you need to transform and exceed customer service expectations. When you execute the process successfully, 100% of the time, you will build an economic firewall, regardless of whether the economy is in a downward tailspin or a pandemic. You must take the long-range view of retaining the customer for a lifetime based on a strong, faultless, over-the-top experience; That is the type of effort that must be a buy-in by all to create this long-term relationship.

Research shows that customers leave businesses because of poor service. On the other hand, customer retention is a natural by-product of great service. The secret is, you have to be obsessed with delivering an over-the-top customer service experience. Another retention matter is consumers are living in a busy world, and timely handled matters build a relationship of trust that is honest and provides that warm and fuzzy feeling. We now understand why customer retention is so critical; we have new customers giving us a try from word-of-mouth marketing, which comes steadily from social media referrals. The impact has to be precise to engage consumers enough to come back again. It has to be relevant, authentic, and professionally executed by cast members, so the consumers come back, again and again, looking for a magical experience.

Chapter 5

Delivering the Master Plan, "The Auto Killer Business Plan"

"Times and conditions change so rapidly that we must keep our aim constantly focused on the future."

"Of all the things I have done, the most vital is coordinating those who work with me and aiming their efforts at a certain goal."

"It is kind of fun to do the impossible."

–Walt Disney

Customer service is the key driver, and, without a doubt, this is the number one issue you have to score big in. It is the most important factor; in fact, it is a critical element that will determine your dynamics with consumers, which drive a business from being 'above average' or 'good' over to 'elite'. Every single interaction you engage in needs to bring the magic. Your words, actions, and energy must be powerful and delivered in a positive, upbeat manner, with 100% tuned-up focus on the consumer and listening as they share their concerns without interrupting them. Then nail down the repair order, so no outstanding concerns or issues are going forward.

Your customer service should be so amazing that it should not make the consumer feel the need to do business with anyone but you! Personalizing your interactions and making the consumer feel important will set your career ahead of others; That is the secret in a nutshell. To achieve this lofty goal, your team needs to own the customer service experience and the power of the service moment. The whole team needs to hold each other accountable for predictability, consistency, efficiency, creativity, sincerity, and excellence to win the day(s).

I believe you can do this. I am challenging you to risk your future and bet on yourself to become a future owner of a business. Start right now; it is a journey with a learning curve. If you dare to dream bigger, you can become an owner of multiple automotive businesses. Put your heart and soul into it, apply this amazing insight, and become one of the next gurus of this amazing industry. Continue to grow by taking in all the secrets this book offers you. Remember, knowledge is power IF you use it in the right manner.

Delivering All the Goods 100% of the Time

The biggest room in the auto service business is the "room for improvement." It is about how you conduct yourself and how you interact with your guests. Use of correct language and common but special terms should make your guests feel very special and much appreciated. On the exit, after the consumer has reviewed the invoice, explain the warranty, share what is recommended that still needs attention, and schedule the next appointment at this time. These are all key steps.

Scheduling appointments for around 65 to 75% of each day affords additional time to slow things down and do it right the first time. This will provide opportunities to share and point out items that need attention as well as follow the manufacturer's scheduled service interval. Print out this document and hand it to the consumer and explain it thoroughly. In the meantime, you can also discuss with the consumer any further opportunities to up-sell and cross-sell to prevent issues down the road.

When you interact with the customers say things like,

"Mrs. Jones, thank you for allowing me the opportunity to serve you today. It is always my pleasure to assist you with your auto needs. I appreciate you as our client; it is always nice to see you. I want to assure you that if you ever need anything, I am here to look after you, and I will go out of my way to provide you with a memorable service experience."

Mrs. Jones will be thrilled by your kind words. It is all part of owning the moment.

During my consulting years, I used to have chit-chats with all the cast members during a provided lunch in the boardroom to discuss matters, so we were all on the same communication level. I would shut off the lights, and the room would go dark. During this time, the question would be asked, and I'd turn on the lights. The question would be, "How many of you believe it is important to satisfy the consumer? Raise your hand if you believe this is indeed true?" In 99% or more of the cases, everyone puts up their hand.

Let us bring reality into sharper focus; various studies indicate that 60-70% of consumers who identified themselves as "satisfied" customers do not necessarily come back. For one reason or another, they are just so-so satisfied. If you had created the 'wow' moments, the moments of magic or little extras, offered a smile, shared the item, used educating versus selling, provided service at no charge, or a complementary quick DVI from Auto Serve1 and Hunter Engineering Quick Check wheel alignment documents in a professional business-like manner, this definitely would have won the day. You, as cast members, need to be dedicated to bringing auto service to a new and higher level by breaking out of old habits (such as saying, 'Have a nice day'). If you asked most of these guests, "How did we do today?" a large percentage would respond with, to quote an amazing author Shep Hyken, whom I respect:

"You cannot be satisfactory because satisfactory is a rating – it is right in the middle is average- how do you like your haircut- it is fine. Fine is like the "F" bomb of customer service. We have to keep our customers for life. If we focus on the NEXT time EVERY time, ultimately we would create a LIFE-time of loyalty."

Every consumer is looking for that ultimate customer experience. "Did we achieve this, did we 'wow' and deliver a memorable event, and was the consumer feedback survey a reflection of an excellent score of 5?" These are the questions a service consultant must ask themselves. If you want to blow your customer's socks off, the experience must be over the top, above and beyond. This will bring them back the next time and the next time. Here are some of the metrics: deliver the ultimate experience with a touch of magic, this has to be the best retention tool, eliminate the churn rate while removing the pain points; if you sense something went off the track, do not hesitate to ask or say, 'I messed up, here is what I am going to do to remove the pain. I am sorry.' Offer a sincere apology. Often, that is enough, but if the customer still seems upset, pull a gift card and present it humbly, and assure the guest that you will always be there for them (and the guest will feel the magic). This is not a cost; it is an investment that provides a lifetime value. Value is what the guests desire, it is like a special fix, and that is where the repeat business comes from.

Use the power of amazing benefits and incredible value, use the language recommended based on what the manufacturer's service intervals are (based on mileage and/or time), and print off and explain the importance of doing the maintenance, as it will extend component life, and finally, complement the guest for their continued loyalty. These are some of the secrets that can help create those magical moments.

The Disney parade marshal (service manager) must continue to invest in the cast members. The "parade marshal" can strike up the band, and act as the cheerleader, the encourager, the supporter, and the helper to rally the team while pushing the service bar upward. Outstanding excellence in all areas must be the mantra that drives the competitors crazy; That is the act you and your cast members need to deliver collectively. Always challenge and encourage the cast members to push themselves and their careers to the next level. It is about breeding a culture to focuses on the magical customer experience.

An industry study shows that a 5% increase in customer loyalty can boost profits by 25 – 90%. Another source indicates that providing an over-the-top customer service experience can impact your sales by 2.5%. These are industry data. So, a question that one should consider asking is, 'Why are we not doing a better job? What do consumers value most? Would you personally do business with you?' The data from Disney shows that a 1% increase in customer loyalty translates into millions in revenue.

I know this because in 2013 when I filled in for a service manager, the team was willing to buy into a plan. I, (author), was recruited to fill in for an ailing service manager. After 13 months, we collectively moved a mountain by generating $2.55M in new business in parts and labor in a store that was already in the top 25% quartile. So, be mightily encouraged; IF you use this "Killer business plan," it will be your blueprint for huge gains and a much greater customer experience. There is no extra cost in doing it right, and we can always earn the moments with our thoughtful, kind words and more so with our actions. Here are some statistics of why customers leave: 1% die, 3% move or relocate, 5% seek a new relationship with another company mostly because of family or other strong relationship, 9% exit on price (they weren't made aware of value for reason "X"), 14% leave due to product issues or workmanship, while 68% perceived the attitude of indifference by an employee(s). The service managers must be involved on the front line, with their eyes and ears on high alert, while technicians work in the service bays.

They need to constantly know the pulse, as well as use the time as a teaching moment or moment to acknowledge excellence. Have a meeting and share this information, ask the question, "Would you be happy with a subpar performance?" The answer is "No." To achieve success, we all have to be willing to go to a certain standard whereby we all see the value in it. Doing your part in creating an over-the-top experience, regardless of your function, creates impeccable quality workmanship and an outstanding customer experience; your day-to-day customer service experience responses will indicate very positive, upbeat comments, and, at the time of exit, you can say something like,

"I trust your service experience was memorable (pause for the answer); we, at "X' greatly appreciate your patronage and value you as our guest."

"And we will always be here for you!"

If delivered with excellence and conviction, the customer's body language should speak volumes.

On the customer feedback survey, reflect a response saying,

"We are the best at what we do, and it is consistently and predictably delivered by all cast members."

Do a "task analysis" and check what percentage of consumers have come back in the last six months or over the past twelve months. A customer service industry specialist needs to call and follow up with these customers to obtain necessary feedback and see if the business can be restored, and understand why the relationship went off track in the first place.

During my years of consulting, I undertook this task. It was very invigorating and rewarding. Out of the thousands I called, all consumers seemed shocked and pleasantly surprised and always talked politely. I came across different responses; a small percentage felt things could have been handled better. I invited those to call me and make an appointment; a great percentage strongly committed to returning (maybe returning to this original service provider was made easier by the telephone call); some consumers had relocated;

some were students moving to look for a new job opportunity. On the whole, it was rewarding to see many of the consumers coming back. Addressing their issues provided us with a range of feedback, along with valuable insights as to how to correct and curb the concerns that had been raised and then have a strong and better thought-out approach going forward.

One can learn so much as valuable feedback allows the entire team to better engage and align with consumer feedback. Feedback is valuable in steering us in the right direction and enhancing the overall experience. Ethics is a key element; hard and pushy selling is a one-time thing that causes the consumer to look for the exit door without complaining, and you chase them right into the open arms of your competitors.

This is a model of how you need to conduct yourselves; your actions must speak volumes, and you must engage and align the message with those who pay all the bills. After any unfortunate instance during the day, week, or month, one should take time to debrief it and use this as a coaching and mentoring moment to develop further skills on how to deal with issues going forward. These lessons will make the organization better and stronger. Allow the consumer to have a choice between appointments and walk-ups. Another huge factor to consider is if your location has high visibility and available space. A consumer who wants a quick and fast service can easily approach you to avail of your services and help generate additional traffic, revenue, and opportunities.

The Amazing Auto Killer Business Plan

Today's businesses need to constantly invest in their teams to keep them mentally sharp and way out in front of their competitors.

Five decades of experience across all sectors of the service industry, of which twelve years were spent coaching and mentoring as a consultant, have provided me with much exposure. I realized that with the right proven processes, best practices, amazing solid strategies, along with valued insight, the opportunities are limitless. I believe, without a doubt, that investing and with the right application of what this book offers, will help one to move out of those stagnant periods. If done with excellence, it becomes a firewall regardless of the recession. I believe that the opportunities are unlimited for those who seek them.

Common Sense

Another solid strategy is to get your cast members to re-invest in advanced fine-tuning resources. This manuscript will bring into focus the areas of great opportunities. So often, the cast members are busy and seem to be rushing around to cater to all the consumer's needs. By focusing on the consumer by slowing the process down and having more meaningful discussions and interactions, building a more in-depth personal relationship, it affords you to create the magic that we have been talking about.

The more time you invest in the consumer, the better results are on the other side. After all, the cast members are the face and voice of your brand. Slowing the process down and educating the consumer will pay huge benefits. This high level of service allows the consumer a "Disney-like" customer service experience.

Visionary Leadership

High-level and effective visionary management can mentor the technicians to grow their earning power, which will help attract other technicians they will need as they progress through this exciting growth stage. The AutoServe1 smart digital vehicle inspection adds to this opportunity, as does the Hunter Engineering Unmanned Quick Check Alignment Machine. The Hunter Alignment Machine provides artificial intelligence that reveals tire Tread Edge Integration (tread depth of each groove). If the wheel is out of adjustment, it will offer additional front-end opportunities such as tie rods, sway bar links, ball joints, and additional tire sales. Three out of every ten vehicles have tires that do not meet the industry standard, i.e., they are worn badly, etc. Consumers will purchase tires from the first person who brings this to their attention. The bonus is that 70% of consumers will then also purchase their regular maintenance, seasonal maintenance as well as overdue maintenance, along with missed or declined previous items.

About 25 years ago, we provided a credible paper vehicle-inspection report. My tagline was, "*If you do not inspect, you cannot expect.*" Another coined phrase was, "*It has to be told to be sold.*"

You must educate new hires; you have to look for people who are willing to embrace change. It is the responsibility of the leader to create a special culture where staff members and consumers enjoy the interaction. Moreover, creating a memorable experience by being helpful, user-friendly, and knowledgeable allows staff members to excel in their work. This is the bedrock of one's success. Finally, ask yourself, have you made the emotional connection?

Let your personality and communication skills shine, and make sure to do it with a warm smile.

Provide Credit Approval APP's

Today, you will find many consumers who cannot afford the cost, strictly because of the circumstances, so you have to take a proactive approach. Assist these consumers with a quick credit application, for example, a CTC credit card, with a period of two years to defer the interest and at a minimum payment.

Being proactive is a benefit to capture additional sales, as you are guiding and sharing ways to assist and help the consumer. An alarming 63% of the consumers are unable to handle a repair of $500 (29% of which are required items), and 71% of additional items are declined due to the lack of funds. If you want to do more business, you and your team need to have market tools to handle such situations.

Consumers, in most cases, cannot afford these repairs, it is just the wrong time, but you should have alternative options and solutions at the tip of your fingers, ready to assist them. So be more creative, and it will land you an additional growth potential. 63% is a large chunk of business that you can lose if you are not knowledgeable enough or not at the top of your game.

Team Meeting

Visionary leaders get it; they are always curious about new ideas, smart tools, a success toolbox, and more. They value their team members and often plan lunches, hold contests, and do other team-building exercises.

It is about being creative and taking out time to celebrate successes and acknowledge cast members for staying late and helping the consumer get back on the road. I suggest team leaders plan these events in advance and announce and post updates to keep their cast members abreast of what is coming down the pipe. Ask them to bring ideas, allow input, and acknowledge them, as it is very important to involve the team. It is about a stronger partnership. The more they are involved, the easier it is to bring others along.

Continuous Learning

Great leaders are constantly engaged in some activity. They are great readers, devouring information, googling for things they do not have command over, listening to webinars, and podcasts, reading industry magazines, purchasing industry books, and whatnot. The leader must be reading, evaluating data, and auditing performances. A leader's vision is all about action based on performance; he is all about advancing the soft skill sets. So, once these skills are implemented, reinforced, and repeated, it is all about practicing and polishing while maintaining these skills until they become their habit(s).

A leader has sharp senses as he/she has to always be on high alert. They make sure everything is perfect and working; the waiting room is tidy, and comfortable, with ample daily newspapers and magazines without dog ears. He/she has to be well dressed, take ownership of all issues, including staffing and sales, and be competitive by nature while having the drive and killer instinct to leave no stone from being overturned.

They analyze the market area to know what is happening and are constantly curious about initiating new and better ideas. They rely on hearing to pick up the tone of the customer and assure them with kind words. One of their greatest traits is setting higher standards and holding cast members accountable. Too many managers are frightened to have frank and open dialogues because consumers have extremely high expectations, and the same applies to cast members. Accountability is critical, which is why the customer service experience must be impeccable and memorable in the first place. It should be like a special event.

A team leader is equally empathic toward his cast members. It is exhibited when they pull a service advisor over to have brief discussions on missed opportunities; likewise, if someone has done something exceptionally well, they encourage it and celebrate it. It is the act of encouragement that builds up the entire team, and it rubs off on the consumer eventually.

The customer service has to be exceptional not just for the walk-in customers but also for the ones who share their issues over the telephone. The inbound call must be answered within the first two or three rings. Likewise, a walk-in customer must be greeted within 3 to 4 seconds.

Cast members must be held accountable for the dress code; their uniforms must look sharp, hair should be well kept, beards well-trimmed, facial expression and body language in sync, and their cell phones must be off and in pockets. It is part of the manager's job to track every advisor's performance, regardless of the data. They have to know exactly who is doing well and who needs more coaching and encouragement – this is critical to performance. Auditing the previous day's invoices for missed opportunities, and average tickets, and following up on declined or refused work is a non-negotiable and must be shared with all cast members. Likewise, they have to hold techs accountable for doing a road test on all drivability issues, noise, or other performance concerns and doing the work right the "first time."

Deliver the Magical Experience

You need to measure everything; the top priority is CSI, That is the real tell-tale sign. Every cast member must bring their best game and never lose sight of the commitments that were made. The consumer is who will evaluate your performance.

The cast member has to take ownership; if you erred or misspoke, immediately find the consumer and explain the situation. Go out of your way to recover that guest and work through the process in an accountable manner. You have to do a little extra to show your sincerity; involve the service manager for advice if you have to. Apologize and always be upfront; do not give excuses. The end goal is that the guest must be accommodated; it is all about winning their trust, time and time again, to gain their repeat business. Be user-friendly, pay great attention to details, make sure you use selective language, and stay in your right lane. Record interactions during such a time, such as who was involved, and finally, make sure costs are noted and recorded. The pickup and checkout must be acknowledged as previously stated. Never let a guest leave unhappy, and certainly not until you have sat down to discuss and sort out the details of the issue at hand. This must be done while doing something a little extra, showing you care a great deal by being upfront regardless of the issue or concern. Learn how to recover in these moments. Your continued relationship with a customer must be deepening.

We are living in what is referred to as an experience economy. Doing it right the first time is a must. Today, the more savvy consumers expect a higher quality service experience. Time and time again, customers are willing to pay more for a better overall service experience. The downside of a bad or not great experience is that it results in consumers abandoning your company simply because you did not meet or exceed their expectations. That is why I continue to emphasize that you must continue to invest in preparing staffers. It is all about retention; thus, greater loyalty and satisfaction will result in increased revenue. The secret is in becoming more effective communicators, where you make a clear choice to educate the consumer versus selling them. Do you like to be approached by a saley or pushy service agent? Do you like going back to a service provider the second time? It is annoying. Service managers have to have accountability and manage their moments. When you create benefits and value and deliver the message in a concise and precise manner, you are doing yourself a huge favor. Plus, the consumer will see you as a service superstar who can handle situations and execute at a very high level. The consumer is self-motivated simply because they clearly understand what is in it for them.

When you engage helpfully with fact-based material that makes sense, consumers begin to line up as buyers. The secret is, that we all have to envision the true potential by being equipped and prepared to create a memorable Disney-like experience. If we go above and beyond, the money will follow, and the social media posts will have consumers looking you up to have the same, over-the-top experience. You have to deliver an exceptional and excellent experience that drives your competitors crazy. These Disney standards are executed by well-trained cast members. These are ordinary people who handle being given an extraordinary training program that is achievable and doable with a little extra effort. Applying the principles discussed within these pages will change your life and your future, so you strive to deliver a world-class service culture and create an environment where everyone is having fun, including the consumers. Your service should be outstanding enough to make the customer provide reviews gladly, especially if you have delivered that 'wow' moment. Without question, many service centers are delivering excellent service already; however, with extra effort, they can take it to the next level, so they can create something they may never have considered. Constantly demonstrate courtesy and respect. Be schooled with all the processes and procedures - become a superstar. There is room on the big stage. It is only you that holds you back, so break away from your comfort bubble. Soon, others will be motivated with the same passion and excitement. Be wise by investing in your career, sooner than later. I can assure you the dividends will be rewarding.

Pain Points

You need to re-examine every interaction point, such as answering the phone by the end of the third ring. When the telephone rings beyond that point, the consumer becomes frustrated. Today's consumers are busy people. When a walk-in consumer approaches and stops right in front of you, are you following the 4-second rule to greet and acknowledge them? Many times, the advisors ignore the consumer and do not even have the courtesy to acknowledge their presence. This leaves an unpleasant first impression. Whatever the task might be, it could have been laid aside to greet the customer promptly.

Today's rule is, that you need to and must acknowledge the consumer within four seconds. Even if you are busy gathering information from the consumer in front of you, you can still glance up and smile, nod, and mouth these wonderful and comforting words, "I'll be with you in a minute or two." You ask the consumer you are currently dealing with if you can interrupt to page someone for assistance.

As a consumer specialist, you must remove the pain points within these proven time frames; they will separate you from the rest of the competition. You have to meet the bar of excellence. Re-evaluate and examine all the potential pain points by reviewing each interaction. For instance, it could be a status call to bring the consumer up to speed, or it could be informing the consumer about what is good instead of jumping in and rattling off all the needed things without creating an ounce of value. Little things are also important, as they might be game-breakers. Let me share a personal experience: the consumer was interested in purchasing a set of tires. Instantly, I realized the advisor was a new hire, and his knowledge was very limited. Their conversation, as I observed, went back and forth and seemed cold. Eventually, the consumer indicated that he would purchase those tires.

Just as I was thinking the moment could not have been more awkward, the service advisor looked at the consumer and blurted out, "Do you want to do a wheel alignment?" (No mention of benefits or value.) At that point, I felt I needed to step in. It is the team leader's responsibility to make sure new hires receive the necessary training; many good organizations have a few weeks of training programs to bring the new cast member up to speed, and to have some confidence. So they are equipped to handle the basic information.

Another pain point is, around four or five o'clock during the pick-up point, and having the customers wait for a long time. To better manage this bottleneck, use one advisor to review the repair invoice, share what still needs to be done, explain the warranty, reconfirm the quoted price, including the taxes, and have another clerk handle the ring-through. Take a moment to thank this valuable consumer, by saying something like:

"We appreciate your patronage and value your business, Mr. Brown. Thank you for the privilege of serving and helping you today. Have an enjoyable rest of the day; see you again."

OR,

"Would you like to book an appointment for the items we just reviewed that were previously declined?"

OR

"I will always be here for you."

The lesson is to learn quickly how to avoid the painful pitfalls. I trust as you read this book, it will empower you to be a much more effective leader. Your cast members must be equipped with the right tools (scripts) on par with the learning and educational process; they also need to be strictly professional. Service providers need to be more consistent and, as a team, need to be more predictable to gain repeat business.

The Value of Tires

History indicates that on any given day in the calendar year, three out of every ten vehicles will require tires to be changed out. Using these numbers as an example: out of 40 vehicles, 12 would require tires (4 tires per vehicle) replacement; multiply 12 by 4 = 48 tires for 261 days (excluding Saturdays and Sundays), which brings the total tire sales for the year to $12,528.

The opportunity and potential are amazing. When I use the term "sold," I believe it is an obligation to educate, inform, and explain to the consumers if their tires do not meet the industry standards. The manufacturers of tires have intentionally built a "wear bar" so that the tires that do not meet the safety standard can be replaced. It is solely about educating and informing the consumer about what their driving needs are and whether each tire's characteristic matches their preference or need.

The Hunter Engineering Quick Alignment Check machine provides evidence using smart technology to get rid of all the chatter and clutter, so the consumer clearly understands what is not good based on a document the machine generates. This is brilliant artificial intelligence that makes the service advisor look very knowledgeable. The service advisor has to educate and inform the client what the benefits are of having a wheel alignment, namely that it will extend tire life, and enhance fuel economy by 4 to 6% while removing stress and fatigue. Most consumers do not understand the meaning and the benefits of a wheel alignment. Use the Hunter Engineering model vehicle to explain the tire angles and the benefits of doing a wheel alignment.

In the following chapters, I have shared a formula, an example of the true potential of this amazing tool. Another staggering number is that approximately 40 to 50% of the vehicles will need some steering and suspension components like tie rods, and ball joints, and will have some leaking struts/shocks as well as leaking power-steering hoses. These alarming numbers are worthy of the investment in Hunter Engineering equipment. The financial business model is a no-brainer. Buying this smart equipment will drive your business to remarkable new levels, to become eye-popping, which was never considered before.

Consumers Love Third-Party Smart Tools

Investing in artificial intelligence, such as Hunter Engineering Unmanned Quick Check Drive and Tread Edge Integration, captures autonomous alignment inspection and edge wear detection while measuring camber, total toe, and tire tread depth on every vehicle while also generating electronic and printed results in seconds. Another smart tool and investment is the AutoServe1 Smart tool like the Digital Vehicle Inspection report. AS1 exposes opportunities that have proven that the additional potentials are real. It moves the consumer to a comfortable position by educating them so that the buy-in is easy, it is reassuring, and it provides a realistic and comfortable state of mind that allows people to realize that it is the right choice. These smart tools remove the all too often grudges that service advisors and consumers feel. These tools accomplish what humans can adequately relate to.

How can you not invest in something that impacts consumers in such a positive way? It is about the decision, the numbers, and the results that get the buy-in from the banker as well. Looking back, You will think, why did we not do it sooner? The financial business plan model demonstrates the true potential that it generates. The Business Model reveals it is not a cost; rather, it is an investment that generates brilliant growth and the potential payback extended over ten years is amazing.

The Future

The global automotive aftermarket industry was expected to reach $722.8 billion or more by 2020. Today's consumers are keeping their vehicles longer and are more aware of the importance of preventive maintenance and scheduled servicing to maximize the lifetime value of their vehicles. This rising demand for aftermarket parts and services is spurring new growth and revenue opportunities for a wide range of businesses operating in the automotive aftermarket industry.

A typical car on the road in the U.S. is a record-high 11.5 years old, according to a new IHS Automotive survey. However, while cars on the road may be aging, consumers are continuing to purchase new vehicles. In 2015, U.S. car sales hit a record high when automakers sold 17.5 million cars and light trucks, which was 5.7% more than the previous year.

Although Americans (and Canadians) may be buying newer vehicles, do not let these numbers fool you into thinking the aftermarket is stagnant or declining. Older vehicles simply last longer. According to a 2015 article by USA Today, "The number of vehicles on the road that are at least 25 years old is about 14 million. That is up from about 8 million in 2002. Those are vehicles made in 1990 or earlier. Meanwhile, the number of vehicles that are 16 to 24 years old is 44 million. That is up from 26 million in 2002, according to HIS."

The Takeaway

The mindset, culture, and vision must capture the hearts and minds of the consumer; from the management down to the front-line service managers and techs, no one should compromise on the goals, vision, and mission statement at any cost. The quality of delivering "above and beyond" the customer experience by front-line cast members must embed the values that will continue to shape the long-term process of consumers falling in love with the world-class experience. That must be the goal and purpose, to continue to grow the double-digit traffic year in and year out and raise the bar that your competition cannot match. Management must have the mental toughness and the "killer instinct" within their attitude to settle for nothing less than excellence in the team's performance that will blow the socks off the customer by delivering the ultimate 'Wow' experience. It is about the training and commitment to adopting the Disney philosophy. We ask for the high standard of excellence that Disney delivers every day. Investing in this type of training that Disney has in its culture will help your team do better and set the pace for even greater success.

You, as a leader, need to set goals to make sure your team exceeds all the expectations of the customers.

Acknowledgement: *Material used in following chapters, 6 and 7, titled 'Delivering Ultimate Customer Experience' and 'Digital Inspection Platform Experience', respectively, obtained from the website of AutoServe1, has been used with permission. A permission letter stating the consent to use this material, obtained from Jamie Cuthbert, CEO and Founder of AutoServe 1, has been attached and can be found in the appendix section of the book.*

Chapter 6

Delivering the Ultimate Customer Experience

"There is only one boss; the customer."

Sam Walton

Digital Inspections with Picture Proof

BOOST TRUST AND SALES

Retail

Fleet

TRUST GAP

- 66% of motorists do not trust auto repair centers in general.
- 73% Claim the #1 reason is that they feel they were recommended unnecessary repairs.

*AAA Survey – 12/2016 Most U.S. Drivers Leery of Auto Repair Shops

- 61% of motorists approved additional work when their advisor used a tablet.

*JD Power- 08/2016 - Vehicle Owners Expecting Connected Service Experience

HOW TO BECOME EXCEPTIONAL DELOITTE RESEARCH

MARKET TREND

WOMEN – THE NEW MAJORITY.
Decide how money is spent.
Employed full time.
Not mechanically trained.
Want to understand.

Delivering Ultimate Customer Experience

MARKET TREND

VEHICLES ARE BUILT BETTER

Repair was easy to sell but dropping.

Maintenance is growing. Harder to sell.

Educate customers about

inspection findings.

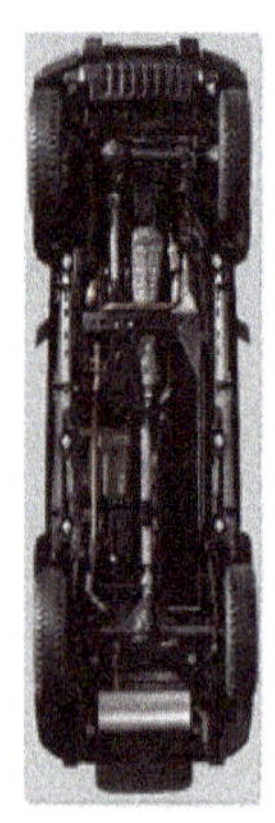

MARKET TREND

TECHNOLOGY ACCELERATION

Fastest growing sector is the Millennials (18-35 yrs).

Tech savvy – multimedia

Information Driven & Sharing Community

MARKET TREND MILLENNIALS

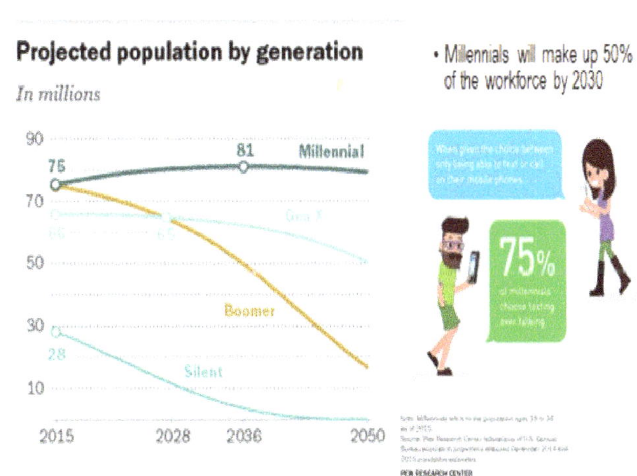

REVENUE IMPACT OF USING AS1

AutoServe1 Revenue Impact on 600,000 invoices, 200 shop sample

Inspection Status	Average Invoice	Dollar Change	% Impact
No AS1 inspection	$418	Baseline	0
AS1 Inspection	$511	$93	22%
AS1 Inspection + Sent to Customer	$564	$146	35%

CURRENT CUSTOMER EXPERIENCE

ULTIMATE CUSTOMER EXPERIENCE

Let me buy vs being sold to

(Change the selling of auto service)

Communicate clearly.
Educate me – don't push me.
Respect me – don't talk down to me.
Let me choose to work with you.

AutoServe1 · Private and Confidential

ATTRACT THE RIGHT TEAM

Technicians communicate all findings professionally

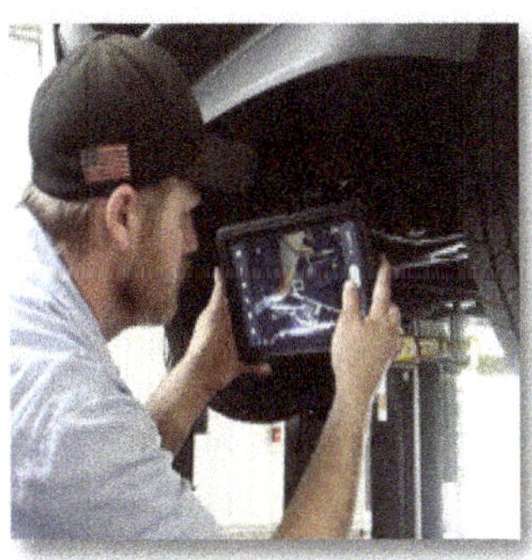

AutoServe1 · Private and Confidential

Manage workflow easier

Give tools to improve shop workflow and communication

AutoServe1 - Private and Confidential

Choosing the right DVI for you

1. Is it easy to implement?
2. Does it integrate?
3. Will customers understand it?
4. Will team use it?
5. Is it proven?

AutoServe1 - Private and Confidential

Gone are the days of rattling off the laundry list. The days of high-pressure selling and driving the business down the road right into the arms of your competition are gone. That is a sure way of giving a possible lifetime consumer (calculate the cost, the real cost) to your competition because they will have done exactly what you failed to do. You sold them to your competition because you failed to communicate effectively; you didn't involve them nor follow the slide messages.

In my consultant experience, I forged a rewarding career that captured the attention of four of the five top executives from a large enterprise known as Canadian Tire (similar to the Pep Boys chain in the USA) to travel to Saskatoon, Saskatchewan. They flew out to our store to engage in how I consistently drove double-digit numbers year after year, wanting to glean and extract the secrets that continued driving a business with only 18 service bays in a small city. With a lower door rate than most, it became the top auto service center out of approximately 500 stores.

Then, I took those lessons into the consultant career that allowed many other stores to win "lottery tickets" that keep on generating revenue year after year. The first store I visited turned into the single best store in the chain. The claim to fame for this dealer was to give me a call to bring a fresh set of eyes to a stale situation. It was already a good auto center, but it was stagnant, and I took this store from good to elite. Dave Malcomson, the associate dealer, and Adam Stuart, who had no or little experience and learned some hard lessons early in his career, shaped these amazing achievements and became the new star with a few more follow-up visits. I am sharing this unique story because it is worth the encouragement to the reader of this information. Thanks to the many others who have spurred me on as well. Ian Van Norman, the first dealer I worked for, after his retirement 37 years later, encouraged and inspired me enough to move forward.

After his retirement, a young Dave Deplaedt arrived in Saskatoon, curious as to whether or not he would be able to have some involvement or any input into his auto service department. Since I had a persona of having considerable success, he showed some concern and wondered if I would be open to him having some input into this side of his business. Of course, absolutely. (I am not sure if that was the exact wording, but I will go with that for now). Of course, I was always open to that. To his credit and his intelligent input, the fantastic ride kept going forward, which was awesome, to say the least. Our discussions were always on the same page and allowed both of us to expand our insights, knowledge, and careers to continue to push and accelerate new growth. Dave was excellent at writing and sending encouraging notes, which made me more determined to be open-minded in reaching constant new sales records.

I share this journey to jolt the readers, owners, and cast members to take these powerful and impactful tools and implement them into their stores, immediately, if not sooner. Why? Because I desire to elevate leadership to encourage the cast members by breaking the old mold/habits and casting new habits. In this situation, I want to motivate you, challenge you, and stretch you to do more, so you can become more. There is a reward for you at the end. I want you to be emotionally and passionately involved in the journey because you can achieve much more.

In this chapter, there is a lot of mention of the 'digital vehicle inspection' (DVI) process. It is powerful, insightful, and impactful. Read on because the proof is in the pudding, or, in today's terms, we have to bake the 'cake' with all the right ingredients measured out precisely, mix in the right processes and finish with the baking, then add the frosting and sprinkle magic to add appeal, which makes the presentation great. It could win the prize money, and you could take home the trophy and thus receive the acclaim of the audience, to which an applause and drum roll is played out. Bring out the band and play the famous tune.

I am deliberately using this analogy because we all have our operations to consider. I am talking like this to create the right atmosphere and magic, pull all the stops, and have the 3 o'clock parade begin, everything on time. Band marshal needs to lead the way in making memorable memories for those needing a magical touch. We have that opportunity to build sincere magic full of fun and surprises, making the consumers fall in love with your brand by applying the elements and the effort in creating an environment that has quality, effective, and knowledgeable people going out of their way to make the experience pleasurable, enjoyable, and memorable.

This happened because we did it differently and added a touch of class to make these consumers willing to share their wallets, while the business and cast members have made a great effort to make them feel special and appreciated. That should be doable and actionable; as the saying goes, "If we can dream, we can do it." If we do things differently and better, it will drive our competitors a little squirrelly.

Five Reasons You Must Always Be Willing to Text Vehicle Inspections

The days of scribbling and presenting greased-up vehicle inspections are over. (This is not meant to hit on great technicians). It is tough keeping them clean and presentable. This was a tool of the past, and its history did serve a purpose. Nowadays, however, more and more shops are embracing the option of texting vehicle inspections. You do not have to feel left out. The numbers support these new and professional processes. Now, there is a best practice in the making!

With AutoServe1's niffy two-way texting feature, you can text customers directly about job approvals, invoice reviews, and updates on repair jobs; you may even text your customers about work that you think they should get done. In addition, the software stores all the conversations and images so that you may refer back to them for any reason. This is powerful stuff!

The ease of communication between the customer and the auto shop is unmatched with the two-way texting feature. However, if you still need convincing, here are five reasons why you should be texting inspections.

1. It Saves Time for Both You and the Customer

Both you and the customer are busy. With a two-way texting feature, You will be able to speed up your job approval process by relaying problem areas to the customer in real time. The customers will save time by not having to come into the shop or answer phone calls. Instead, they can simply approve the repairs to be done, quickly from wherever they are, without taking much time out of their already busy lives. Customers are said to reply to a text five times faster than if you had called them and left a message. Therefore, it is clear customers appreciate this time-saving feature.

2. It Builds Customer Trust and Loyalty

Unfortunately, some animosity and mistrust often exist between auto shops and customers when a customer brings in a vehicle to fix one thing and, upon returning, is told of many other problems that need fixing. The best way to squash this animosity, and mistrust and build loyalty is by texting them the pictures or videos, explaining what you found while working on their vehicle. The photos highlight the problems so that the customers can see them for themselves (in real time), which means they will trust your suggestions. By trusting your shop and, thus, seeing you as honest, You will build customer loyalty.

3. It Appeals to Tech-savvy Millennials

Millennial drivers are quickly becoming a significant portion of drivers on the road today. In 2016, Millennials purchased 4.1 million vehicles, accounting for 29% of the market. Millennials are known to be very tech-savvy, and so digital inspections will indeed appeal to them. In addition to that, Millennials do not like phone calls and voicemails. If they have the option to communicate with you via text, they would gladly take it. Millennials are already hard to keep as customers, so employing this feature and digital inspections, on the whole, will make them feel catered to. Good customer satisfaction will lead to good online reviews, and then more customers will come flocking to your auto shop. It is a win-win.

4. Young Drivers Will Learn a Lot

Millennials are quick to own cars; however, their knowledge of cars isn't growing quite as quickly. Research suggests that 60% of Millennials have not attempted to repair, modify, or fix their vehicles in any way. With the feature's ability to send videos and photos explaining clearly what is wrong and why it needs to be fixed, Millennials will learn more about auto repair. They will appreciate that you are the one teaching them. Again, good customer satisfaction among Millennials will lead to referrals and good reviews.

5. Your Customers Will Be Safer

Safety is typically a top priority for customers. They are more likely to approve more service jobs when digital inspections are used. The average repair order goes up by 15%.

By default, customers driving cars with fewer problems are driving safer cars, which They will appreciate. Customers will also have peace of mind driving, knowing they and their families are in a safe vehicle.

What are you waiting for? Ask us how you can improve your customers' lives through the two-way texting system offered with our digital software.

Finally, a Digital Vehicle Inspection program will provide you with smart, empowering, and educational insight that shares excellent information whereby consumers sell themselves.

Ask yourself, why are you not googling AutoServe1 (DVI)? Their leasing program means there is zero upfront cost. The amazing and easy-to-use software generates a fantastic uptick in sales, driving the profit margins and making consumers feel empowered. As a reader, I trust the upside of this innovative tool is something you will seriously consider. I wish I had had this option during my career. It has so much to do with helping your business thrive: from changing a good auto center into an elite auto center. This is a no-brainer, a must-have. The financial impact is what C.E.O.s and owners are always talking about. My suggestion is to make the call; you have zero to lose and so much to gain! Do not delay; it is the very best tool to inject new life into the future of your business.

Let us examine the technician's pay scale: most enterprises hire at a "per piece of work" rate or "flat" rate. By using this tool, they would work on fewer cars and become more efficient and productive, thus taking home more pay. I believe this would be like working smarter rather than longer. Just look at the numbers! Could there be an increase in wages or a bonus? Slow things down and invest in some re-training to advance and upgrade to new skills. The O.E.M.s, manufacturers, and dealerships have technicians do upgrades outside the workplace. Today, I would expect all of it to be online. Their agreement allows for techs to do warranty work and have this certification. Regardless, dealership or aftermarket service center training is essential. Consumers want it fixed right the first time. That is a given. This will reduce the ugly churn monster from entering your service department. This damages the business in many cases. Yes, this involves everyone in the service department. Listening and recording information is critical. Communication must be clear, concise, and precise. We have to repeat it back so we can clean it up. Many of these errors come from bad habits not being replaced with best practices. Gentlemen and ladies, I want to be realistic.

There is a popular coined phrase that says, "We hire for attitude and train for skills."

I am writing about going above and beyond the call of duty in creating and enhancing an environment driven by creative, elevated, and visionary leadership [manager(s)] that is willing to inspire and lead others in becoming more engaged.

During my career and in my role as a consultant, there came a time when a service center became stale and stagnant. In this environment, one needed an injection to bring new energy, ideas, approaches of the best practice, proven processes, more effective strategies, and insights to release successful tools that would produce more effective results. When we fine-tune an operation, the numbers will be phenomenal. Shop owners should be encouraged to reread this cutting-edge material. We all want to be winners. When we do it right the first time, we win more. All cast members need to step up to the challenge by applying the materials within these pages.

Service managers need to be involved in the daily routine of the frontline cast members. It is about reinvesting, refocusing, retraining, re-motivating, re-challenging, and holding the team accountable to the consumer by enhancing the service experience.

This requires investing in new cutting and advanced materials to stay ahead of the competitors — the three L's stand for **'Life Long Learning.'** As a result, managers back away from old habits and become more resourceful, resilient, impressive, and willing to try new approaches.

I encourage the entire cast members to revisit processes, best practices, and proven strategies and treat guests like VIPs (very important people) since they will share their wallets when we create Model moments of magic that make our guests very happy.

Stunning Vehicle Reports Raise Trust and Revenue. This smart tool is a winner!

Revenue Impact of Using a DVI program.

Data: DVI Revenue Impact on 600,000 invoices from 200 shops. (Outstanding sample size).

No Inspection: Average Invoice	$418
Average Baseline Impact	0%
DVI Inspection: Average Invoice	$511
Average Dollar change	$93
GAIN	22%

DVI Inspection + sent to the customer via text:

Average Invoice	$564
Average Dollar change	$146
GAIN	35%

Here is the possible impact. All things being equal, the investment into DV1 is a win.

Let us do the math on 5,000 invoices @ $93 = $465,000 sales x 10 years = $4,650,000

Let us do the math on 10,000 invoices @ $146 = $1,460,000 sale x 10 years = $14,600,000

Let us explore the difference of 13%. So my question is: what would be implemented in a best practice, epic strategy, and proven process? Business investors desire the best possible return on investments (ROI). This is definitely about forming a new habit because the proof is in the numbers. Let us be frank for a minute. Not texting is shortcutting the process. I have read different authors' articles online and in the service industry's monthly publications on this auto service field, and it is fascinating.

I point to one more piece of valuable information. It is about why one invests in the business, and if you are going to invest in the first place, why would you not you want to maximize your return on investment? Each heading has uncovered potential and real opportunities. I want to address stuff you will be excited about taking to your banker. Let us look at the margin percentile. Here are the goods, the real reveal and tell on how we performed. This applies to everyone in every business, province, and prefecture (Japan). Regardless of the country, this model is fundamentally sound. Margins are significant, and I can assure you that every owner will side with me and applaud this, and rightfully so.

Financial Business Model Impact

Let us examine and explore numbers as related to New sales.

New sales of 5,000 invoice @ $93 = $465,000 sales x 10 years = $4,650,000.

$465,000 times 25% margin = $114,000

Additional profits based over a 10-year continuous business pattern = $1,162,500.

Let us look at a business model using 10,000 Invoices @$146 = $1,460,000 x 30% = $438,000 sales x 10 years = $14,600,000 additional profits

Based over a 10-year continuous business pattern = $4,380,000.

That is a great return on ROI.

Regardless, the Digital Vehicle Inspection is quick and easy to operate; it creates trust at the point of decision; it is not a cost but a return on investment, the software of which will continuously be upgraded. Look at the numbers; it is a solid investment. This is a solid blueprint for wealth. Shop owners invest in buildings, computers (with software breakdowns and issues), hoists, wheel alignment equipment, and air compressors (into heating, lighting, and electrical energy; these are monthly fees). Leadership and other cast members like technicians, apprentice training, oil and lube, and tire guys happen to be the annual single highest cost of any line on one's balance sheet, or P&L. Let me encourage you to exercise mental fortitude to break down old habits while using the same mental power to enhance new habits.

I strongly recommend you visit the AutoServe1 website and visit their testimonials section. Folks, it is a win-win for the consumer and your business. Stop and Google it. It is amazing. It will blow your mind!

CHAPTER 7

DIGITAL INSPECTION PLATFORM EXPERIENCE

What the world needs now more than ever is people to lead through change, now is the time to learn – and exemplify leading through change.

"Marketing without data is like driving with your eyes closed."

– Dan Zarella (Social Media Scientist)

Using the right technology, like the Auto Servel Digital Vehicle Inspection Report, provides the right and stunning information to dialogue with the consumer. The objective of doing this digital inspection is to determine the vehicle's overall condition, roadworthiness, and safety concerns. In other words, it is to check whether the vehicle is road-worthy and safe to drive, or whether will it lead to additional costs such as towing, having to rent another vehicle or hotel bills, or missing an important engagement, especially that with a family member. Utilizing the latest technology is like having a complete health check, like that of your heart, from a cardiologist. Such powerful tools will work on your behalf, help persuade and influence customers with visible data confirmation, thus providing additional upselling opportunities for your benefit and well-being and will increase the overall value of your ARO ticket.

Again, I am talking about what needs to be addressed. Selling is part of it; however, the bigger part is about empowering our guests by educating them. Technology is more effective, impactful, and user-friendly as compared to the hard-sell approach. It is not a cost. Instead, it is an investment tool for creating trust at the point of decision because it allows consumers to educate themselves. The proof is in the number that AutoServe1 generates; it shows truly an amazing increase of 22%.

I believe every service advisor, regardless of experience, should attend a one-day Preventive Maintenance refresher course from their supplier, as well as reading the chapter on "How to Deliver a Million-dollar Opportunity" to have their eyes re-opened since the industry is evolving and chemicals are improving and becoming more effective. New and all other frontline cast members need to embed the amazing benefits and incredible value of Preventative Maintenance in their minds. Things are constantly changing! We have to stay updated with the times. The word tracks and scripts need to be read, re-read, practiced, re-practiced, polished, re-polished, memorized and re-shared with a co-worker until they flow perfectly with the right tone and with confidence and body language. All advisors must understand the science behind the chemicals that are used, and they must see firsthand the before-and-after results. Seeing is believing. It is powerful and will transform their approach to recommending services based on the manufacturer's service interval schedule.

This is a must-have in every cast member's success tool kit. I strongly believe you have to invest in the most advanced AI or smart devices for one purpose: to enhance the customer service experience. It is the single best investment that will generate an unbelievable return on investment, be it AutoServe1 or Hunter Engineering. The positive and stunning financial business models are the final proof.

When you face resistance or outright objections from customers for recommending a Preventative Maintenance service, your knowledge about the technology will help you create value. Many times I have observed service advisors helping customers purchase a set of tires. The customers want to know how many kilometers to expect from the tires. Sadly, the advisors would do nothing to educate the buyers, nor would they emphasize the benefits and actual value-added. There would be no mention of after-care, such as rotations or checking the tire pressure regularly. They might ask to perform an alignment, to which the customer's answer would be "No."

I blame these awkward scenarios directly on the lack of accountability of some service managers, the result of which is lost sales or customers looking for the exit door. Statistically, 60% to 65% of vehicles on the road need wheel alignments at any given time (according to Hunter Engineering data); this may be the single highest failure rate in the auto service industry that goes unchecked.

Visit the scrap tire recycling compound and examine the tires' DNA. Many of the consumers never receive full value on their tires. They become churn customers who then leave and seek out another service provider. Due to no follow-up, no valuable feedback, and no retention, you have sent them right into your competitor's arms. If your staff is not capturing a conversion rate of 35% of the wheel alignment business, you are failing yourselves and your clients. I would go out on a limb and indicate that 65 to 70% of consumers fail to get full value on their tire purchases. This is sad; the proof is there; like I continue to say, it is about educating the consumer. That is our job, responsibility, and obligation. Nothing is better than the digital approach. This should not be seen as a cost but as a wise investment strategy to increase the average repair ticket. Technology is a powerful sales tool because it is believable and professional when educating the customer. If I were still in the business, I would jump in with both feet to adopt these latest technologies. Consider the autoserve1.com. website. I am sold on it and wholeheartedly endorse it. Take a trial offer and watch it work for your customers.

The auto service industry is driven by information like this. I witnessed the power of technology personally when I filled in for a critically ill service manager. I saw wheel alignments grow from under 489 annually to over 2500 in about thirteen months. The technology was justified as an investment (not as a cost) and paid for itself within a few months. In addition to wheel alignments, there was a 40% increase in additional required work from the steering and suspension areas, such as tie rods, ball joints, sway bar links, struts, shocks, and power steering hoses. The third-party colored print-outs, according to Hunter Engineering data, show that 50% of the vehicles require wheel alignment adjustments and need attention right away. This technology helps the techs, the advisors, and the manager see the huge business potential/opportunity, with higher retention and great satisfaction. A continuous growth record, year after year, is also positive proof. Having a glance at the amazing document, you can see that the tires shown in green color were good, while the red color means to stop or danger; thus, sharing these findings with the consumer assured them of an independent third party that their vehicle needed attention.

This makes buyers feel at ease and comfortable about the need to do a wheel alignment. I sincerely believe that it is necessary to further educate the consumer on the benefits and what value it brings, i.e., it extends the life of tires, thus achieving closer to the actual manufacturer's recommended rating. Furthermore, the alignment brings the vehicle back to the manufacturer's specs which will improve the fuel economy by 3 to 7%, as well as help reduce the emission of green gases, and finally, eliminate the stress and fatigue of the steering components such as the tie rods. Digital Vehicle Inspections (DV1) technology is another smart tool that educates the consumer on what is good, as well as what needs attention and what is recommended.

This technology removes the grudge purchase as photos, videos, and educational clips provide a level of education and comfort. Hunter Engineering Company's Quick-Check system and its Wheel Alignment machine are the way of the future. These impressive smart tools provide persuasive visual arguments to consumers, but not everyone has adopted them yet. Hunter Engineering Company has an impressive graphic on its website that shows the ROI for such technology, as the potential for profit growth in the immediate future is often overlooked.

I provided a financial business model for over ten years. It is easy to look at this technology as an expensive item, but the increased efficiency it provides results in higher AROs that argue compellingly for this investment. Technology is a remarkable tool to retain customer loyalty, for customers who might otherwise not return for business, and re-enforces value, which results in eliminating buyer's remorse.

Consider what award-winning auto technician and instructor Pete Rudloff has to say about DV1 in "The Digital Decision" (July 12, 2018, on autoinc.org) quote:

"I spent the first few years of my career as a flat-rate tech whose primary job at a local dealership was to fix broken transmissions and handle complicated diagnostics, much of which was warranty work. Any tech that has worked on a flat rate at an OEM dealer knows that living on warranty work is a hard way to make hours.

"Early on, I had to learn not just how to be efficient at diagnosing and repairing complex systems but also how to efficiently evaluate every vehicle, every time, so that some non-warranty work could be presented to the vehicle owner. Brakes, suspension, tires, lights, wipers, and similar items were vital points to check because these repairs were not reimbursable under the manufacturer's warranty and, as such, paid better to repair.

"I honed my skills and became efficient at finding everything that was not right on a vehicle, a profitable endeavor that I carried with me when I ventured out into my journey as a shop owner. Nineteen years later, I am sure that one of the cornerstones for my continued success has been the inspection processes I created before I was a shop owner and have refined ever since." Unquote.

DV1 has great merit because it provides clients with an immediate snapshot of what is good and then allows a transition (without surprise) to what needs immediate attention so customers can think about their budgets. The photos or videos can be sent via a cell phone, text, or email, which lends greater credibility to the recommendations. A big part of vehicle ownership is having confidence in the efficacy and reliability of any repair investments.

The single biggest reason to buy into DV1 is the powerful impact it has on vehicle owners. They can read a report with pictures or videos as real-time proof of their vehicle's health status. It helps owners feel good about discussing the need for necessary repairs and puts the customer at ease when making that investment. If the shop presents a thorough list of what is either in good condition or in need of attention, the owner will respond positively.

Shops using DV1 will see a solid ARO increase of 35% after switching over. Even if they only see 10% to 15% increases, the outcomes are worth it. Just a quick review of the financial business model over one year is amazing; the model also provides a projection of the impact on the P&L statement while projecting a picture of the greater impact over ten years.

Another positive aspect of going the DV1 route is that it helps a business perform consistent inspections on every vehicle that goes through the shop. While the same can be accomplished with a paper inspection, it does not have the instantaneous effect of DV1. The paper inspection is less credible and sometimes difficult to read. Plus, the information is easier to save, locate, and retrieve at a later date with any accompanying notes of concern. The uniformity will also keep the tech from jumping ahead or skipping items. DV1 will save time since the vehicle needs only be lifted once. The estimate can be given to the customer quickly – That is the inventory we're selling: time. It improves shop absorption, productivity, and labor efficiency.

To summarize, DVI results in higher ARO, and net profit increases, and the well-organized details impress clients who are put in a positive mood when they are shown all the items that do not need work. This makes it much easier to discuss the items that do need attention or will need it soon. It is professional and shows you are not a hole-in-the-wall grease monkey shop but a high-tech, educated auto repair facility.

Here is a comparison of digital inspection versus paper inspection:

Digital Inspection Software

- Reports are available in seconds for review by techs, advisors, and customers.
- Clean and legible. It makes the report look clean and professional when presented to the customer.
- Inspection reports can be sent and viewed quickly on the customer's phone or email.
- Provides photo evidence of the vehicle's condition to inform the client in a better way.
- Tracks maintenance statistics of all inspections.
- Built-in maintenance schedules.

Paper Inspection Forms

- A filing system needs to be implemented, which makes it challenging to retrieve reports.
- Messy handwriting, scribbles, or stains make the report look unprofessional.

- Techs may "pencil whip" through the report to save time.
- Long response time for inspection reports to get to the customer and back.
- It cannot provide photo evidence of the vehicle's condition.
- It cannot measure maintenance statistics.
- Techs must consult OEM maintenance schedules on a separate computer.

The right technology goes a long way to reduce buyer remorse and helps junior advisors avoid winging it. At the same time, it also helps all service advisors to become more polished. It is a matter of presenting yourself and your staff as professionals instead of amateurs.

Five Tactics to Boost a Dealership's Service Sales Using DVI

The Problem Facing the Fixed Ops Department

The reality is, that mobile mechanics and affordable aftermarket shops mean most dealerships lose a percentage of their clients, and over some time, as they become much better, they gain a greater share of the market.

You may have a master mechanic on hand, but people are not interested in getting service at the dealership. As the fixed ops department can account for a lot of dealership sales in any given timetable, dealerships must have proper strategies in place to bring in a healthy, loyal crowd to get their required vehicle servicing. To help dealerships reel in some of these customers and sustain a healthy fixed ops department, we have put together a short list of ways they can win back some of these customers through creative and effective strategies that have proven to work.

1) Sell an Experience

Do not just sell your customer the features of a car you are selling. Sell them the benefits and value; education is the better choice! For example, if your customer is a family man, you can explain how the SUV is the ultimate family getaway vehicle for summer fun. The same can be said about selling services. Do not just lay out a bunch of recommended services. Sell them on why they are important. Explain how the tire tread is dangerously low and can put the customer's family in danger if the tire pops at high speeds.

You can explain how if it does not pop in the city, then when the family is set to go on vacation in a few days, they may pop on the road. Nobody wants their vacation ruined because of preventable maintenance. You can say how, if they are going camping, one stick can be the death of the tire, and if they do not have a spare one, they could be stranded in the middle of nowhere (without cell reception!)

The point here is to sell them the benefit of getting the service done now instead of waiting until something happens.

Another thing you can do to go above and beyond for your customers is: you offer unique giveaways. For example, do you know the family has a dog? Send them a dealership-branded dog tag with a note saying how you hope 'Baxter the bulldog' is enjoying his trips to the dog park in his parent's new SUV.

2) Service Financing

Sure, your dealership may finance car sales for customers. But do you offer customers financing on their service repairs? The reality is, that most people cannot afford a large repair without drowning in credit card debt. When your dealership does not offer customized payment options, you are letting those customers slip through your fingers!

3) Reap the Interest Rewards

This is also a great way for dealerships to make a lot more money on service repairs and increase revenue over time. Dealerships can reap the rewards of interest being accumulated onto a sale while giving the customer the repairs they need to drive safely.

Not only can your fixed ops department make more money from the interest (paid), but you also have an easier time upselling customers.

"I'll get to that when I get paid."

As many people cannot shell out a lot of money on unexpected repairs, they often put off pricey work. Just think about it: what if you were in the shoes of a customer who just got told they needed $1000 of repairs? What would sound better to you? $1000 right now to complete the needed repairs or $50 a week for 20 weeks? You would take the latter option. It is also psychological and works in your favor as a smaller figure spread out simply appeals to people more than a lump sum payment. It comes across as less money than it is.

Financing gives advisors an easier time closing bigger sales as well. The unavailability of this option and not being able to afford the service upfront leaves everyone upset. It leaves the fixed ops department without a sale, the customer upset, and their families anxious about an unsafe car.

It also gives the customer the option of going to another shop later. With larger chain stores, such as Canadian Tire in Canada, offering customers financing on repairs, they will simply go where they can get the deal That is right for them.

Auto repair financing solves all of these problems and relieves the pressure of a larger repair order. When you offer to finance, it lets your dealership come off as the best option in the anxious mind of the customer. They are already at your fixed ops department and want their vehicle fixed. This gives you an immediate advantage over other service providers.

When you offer them a flexible payment option, it gives the customer even more reason just to approve the work on a plan.

4) Embrace Technology

It is time dealerships embrace new technology. With so many customers fleeing the dealership for aftermarket shops, something needs to change. What dealerships can do is involve techs in the fixed ops department. As thousands and thousands of aftermarket shops already use techs in the service department, dealerships need to catch up. If a customer can get this kind of service at aftermarket shops, why would they go to a dealership?

The first thing dealerships can do is implement an automated email system. This can do wonders in maintaining a relationship with customers while providing them with value. They can send them email reminders of what needs to be serviced next (based on their manual).

Next, you should begin writing blog posts! You can write posts that would intrigue anyone who drives a car. For example, you can write about "The top 5 best road trip destinations" or write about the importance of regular oil changes; the limit here is your imagination. The goal of writing blogs is to maintain that relationship with customers by giving them valuable insights from experts like you!

Next, your dealership can start a monthly newsletter that can push out all the news happening in your store. You can offer customers your blog post updates on what vehicles you may be getting soon. You can even offer your newsletter subscribers special coupons like "10% off your next oil change!" just to be part of your list. We would also recommend making use of social media and remaining active on it. As more and more Millennials are on the road, you need a way to connect with these people. So, what do you do? You go to where they are! Create social media profiles on all the popular sites, including, but not limited to, Facebook, Instagram, and Twitter.

On these sites, you have the opportunity to engage with customers directly. You can post engaging content (like your blogs!). You can even post "stories" and show your customers what it is like at your dealership on any given day. This is a great way to humanize your brand and a great way to show your awesome personality!

The more followers you get, the better! You can host special promotions on social media where you post an image promoting your fixed ops department and ask people to like/retweet the post for a chance at a free oil change. People love these types of promotions as they enjoy free things.

5) Create Trust with Digital Vehicle Inspections Easy Recording Options Increase Repair Jobs

Technicians can use their smartphones or tablets to easily record their inspection process. Digital vehicle inspections allow the tech to include video and images right into the report. This lets customers see exactly what technicians see every step of the way. It is a real hit with customers as they now feel like they can make better, more informed decisions when approving work. Without this technology, they had to take a mechanic's word for it whenever their vehicle needed work.

When the customer is educated, shops have a much easier time upselling work. Imagine combining the ease of getting customers to approve work with financing options available and informing them with digital vehicle inspection reports.

We conducted a case study where we found that, on average, service centers that used our software had their average repair orders increase up to 25%! When the customer feels like they have a clue of what is going on under the hood and in the minds of techs doing the inspections, they feel like they can make a much better/informed decision when approving work.

Every Step Made Simpler with Workflow1

With the WorkFlow1 feature, you can ensure your shop is always on the same page. From start to finish, this gives your team an at-a-glance progress report of the auto repair process. Service advisors can update the progress of the vehicle with a click of the mouse. They can even let techs know when parts are ready through the software or via text message.

No More Voicemails

The power of digital vehicle inspections means you will not have to wait for a customer to call you or have to deal with annoying voicemails as customers can receive the full inspections on their smartphones, including photos and videos. They can also approve the work straight from their phone.

Optimize Shop Performance

AutoServe1 can let you track important metrics as well. With the revolutionary software, you can see things like tickets created each day, all the inspections done, and even team members' performance. You can track how many jobs each of your techs have completed and can evaluate what areas need to be improved or where they may need more training.

Custom Inspections

Dealers may need to have a completely different inspection process for in-house inspections than for service. If you want different inspections for different parts of the garage, That is also possible. For example, you can have special inspections for your pit stop crew that needs custom inspections for things like tires, oil, and fluids. The AutoServe1 uses amazing technology and stunning documents that provide third-party evidence, which is incredibly powerful. More often than not, it changes the consumer's mindset from a "no" to a "yes." The digital inspection report provides real-time insight into what is good, what is recommended, and what is needed and required. This is brilliant technology as it helps build a relationship of trust between the consumers and the service manager and center staff; they also realize that getting the recommended service done will be beneficial for them from a safety point of view.

The analytical data obtained from over 200 stores and 600,000 invoices proves the credibility of these smart devices and shows that they are not a cost, but rather a great investment. I would advise the auto service providers to do it now, instead of waiting and missing out on additional revenue, and more importantly, missing out on providing great insight in helping the consumer make a wise choice.

The Takeaway [DF]

The smart tools will provide confidence to the consumer and create trust at the point of decision. The data supports increases in Average Repair Orders by 22% with AutoServe1 Digital Vehicle Inspection. Hence, it is well worth the investment.

Acknowledgement: *Material used in the following chapter 8 (Winning Big with Hunter Engineering), in regards to Hunter Engineering, was obtained from Hunter Engineering's website and used with permission. A permission letter stating the consent from Hunter Engineering Co. can be found in the appendix section of the book.*

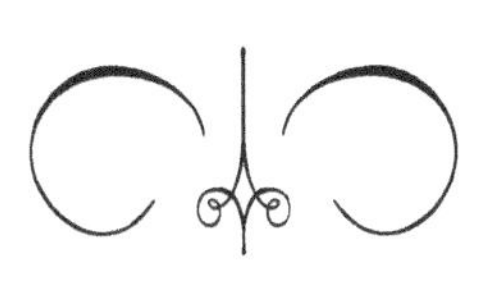

Chapter 8

Winning Big with Hunter Engineering

"Everything rises and falls on leadership."

–Dr. John C. Maxwell

"Knowing who your customers are is great, but knowing how they behave is even better."

–Jon Miller

There isn't a bigger category in any vehicle, nor a bigger revenue opportunity, than the suspension area. Thus, a tremendous sales growth potential is reliant on the failure rate of suspensions. This is one of the crucial chapters in this amazing book, which will provide a major revenue bounce as we advance. Smart artificial intelligence tools similar to Hunter Engineering's Autonomous Quick Check Alignment machine immediately build customer retention and, thus, greater consumer loyalty. It is a win for the consumer as well as for the business and the technicians.

With today's technologies, when we present the Quick Check Alignment document to the consumer and explain what has transpired, one must educate them about the amazing benefits and incredible value, with confidence. I believe that the growth number can reach 50% or greater by prolonging the presentation and educating them. While it is not about selling, it is entirely about educating and, as a result, empowering the consumer so they understand what is in it for them.

Investing in the Hunter Engineering Quick Check Alignment machine (AI) will contribute toward a rapid growth cycle. It is about showing the consumer this amazing illustrative printed document. It immediately serves the purpose, as it impacts the consumer in a significant way. The green-colored wheels' setting shows good news; it is completely neutral from a third-party point of view, with validation that should make the guest feel comfortable and confident. However, when one or more wheels are 'red,' it is like a stop sign.

A picture is worth a thousand words. Without a doubt, it impacts the consumer; it makes reality the top priority. If they haven't completely bought in, the cast member can hand over this amazing document to explain WIIFM. Doing a wheel alignment will extend the life of the tires, increase the fuel economy, and remove stress from the steering components. Moreover, the vehicle will track much better and function more safely, especially in icy and snowy conditions. The consumer needs to hear, visualize, and understand the importance and value of a wheel alignment, which the tire manufacturer supports.

Additionally, vehicle manufacturers recommend and support the maintenance aspects. If the consumer is not buying in, communication may be key to comprehending the obstacles, whether finances or additional repairs. Make sure you make arrangements for quick credit applications. An example would be General Motors, their counterparts and franchise operations, and associate stores like Canadian Tire and their independent service centers and tire shops. Analytic data supports that timing does not always work; they are similar to untimely events and expenses like mortgage, rent, students attending university, etc.

We know the things that cause the issues; the entire team needs to be more proactive. Staff welfare depends on how we deliver the services at every stage. We have to up our game and be more accountable to those who share their wallets with us. Quality of service or product dissatisfaction accounts for 14% of the customers' churn, a direct result of things that are actually in our control. It is about a lack of accountability among team members or a reflection on the manager. The opportunity for additional wheel alignments has tremendous potential, in fact, almost unlimited. Therefore, investment in a Hunter Engineering Quick-Check System has the single largest potential for improved ROI.

Here is another secret. Go back to the discarded recycle tire storage area or bin and have a look. While consulting, I look closely at the condition of each of the tires in this storage. 65–70% of the tires show excessive wear, be it toe or camber, while others were either under-inflated or over-inflated. My point is, that the opportunity is unlimited when it comes to generating additional revenue using wheel alignment check as a starting point.

Here is another amazing secret I wish to point out. The third-party color printout is also a powerful tool to educate your consumers on benefits and value. The Quick Check alignment system requires one to drive through a designated lane, and a mandatory courtesy check of 100% of vehicles 100% of the time. An actual report is generated within seconds, demonstrating your integrity to the customer and making them feel good and comfortable about the process. When you are done, provide them with a copy of the printout.

An example of a word track could be:

"Mr. Jones, we have the technology that can provide you with a quick snapshot of where your wheel alignment is presently at, in comparison to the manufacturer's specs of your vehicle. This is confirmed by the right front tire DNA, which shows extreme tire wear, whether toe or camber.

Today, you invested in a new set of tires, so doing a wheel alignment will increase the full tire life of your purchase and maximize and protect that expensive investment. Is this important to you? The wheel alignment will eliminate the fatigue and stress on expensive front steering components and allow you to reach closer to the manufacturer's 100,000k mileage rating. However, it varies with tire brands and application use. Do you see the value of eliminating the cost of expensive steering components by performing the alignment today?

Your front tire DNA shows evidence that the tire is affected by a wheel alignment out of spec and is a tell-tale sign, causing your vehicle not to track properly as one is traveling down the road. This scrubbing resistance creates great heat and accelerates wear that cuts short the life of your tires and your investment. Performing the wheel-alignment adjustment will also lead to better fuel economy."

This is a powerful benefit. One source (EPA-AA-LDTP78-12) indicates a 4% improved fuel economy; other studies suggest even greater improvements up to 5–7%. You can also add the following:

"Mrs. Jones, would you like to have a better fuel economy and reduce greenhouse gas emissions? Does this make sense? How would you like us to proceed? I'm sure you see the amazing benefits and rock-solid value. This wheel alignment creates immediate savings, plus better and safer handling for your vehicle, which is important to you. The wheel alignment investment is (for example) $109.99, and we can have it completed in the next 45 minutes. Does this work for you?"

Know this script. Memorize it. Be committed to role-playing it with the service manager and flat-out nail it. This will elevate your confidence and allow you, the service advisor, to grow and empower yourself and the consumers. Consumers can read your body language and hear the tone of your voice; it is a quick reflection of your confidence. Turn up your focus to the next level. Improve the tone of your voice and show your confidence through body language. A smile is as important. As we become more aware, things will change for the better, but first, you have to work and start using your memory muscles. Do not fake it. Consumers can see and sense if you cut short the process and are just going through the motions.

The asking part is vital. A great percentage of advisors fail to motivate and educate the consumers to say 'Yes,' to create great value. The situation I commonly encounter is advisors not 'asking', while some are simply blurting out the price. These statements fail the customer's expectations. It is outright shameful that service managers even allow this behavior. They have to train their team members to be more effective and execute the above script as per industry standards. Take the time to coach and empower the team members to have confidence and own the power of knowledge. There is always room for improvement, lots of it.

If you watch the customer nodding and agreeing with your statements, they will often say, *"Go ahead and do it."* When consumers are educated and clearly understand what is in it for them, they are motivated by value and agree to what the advisor recommends to them. Here are a few more industry facts from Tire Business in 2004: a vehicle with the alignment toe just 0.34 of a degree (0.17cm or 1/8 inch) outside of the specification may cause the front tires to scrub sideways, up to 11.5 feet, for every mile driven. If a vehicle has dragged its tires sideways for more than 108 kilometers during a 20,000-kilometer span (close to what the average individual drives in a year), it may reduce the tire life by 25% or more.

Tire Life Extension Facts

One critical factor in tire longevity is heat. A tire wears faster if it gets hotter, caused by scrubbing. Moreover, a tire also gets heated because of friction when alignment is out of spec.

Reducing the heat build-up on the tires requires:

- Proper inflation pressure (see the driver sill or inside driver side door pillar) and rotation play a role in extending value.
- Alignment angles set to factory-spec tolerances.
- Reasonable highway speeds.
- Non-aggressive cornering.

Profit Opportunities

According to Modern Tire Dealer in 2012, here are some profit margins by service:

- Brakes = 52%
- Electronic Diagnoses = 61%
- Balancing = 64%
- Alignments = 65%

Wheel alignment is a quick and easy diagnosis, and there are numerous symptoms. These include loose tie rods and ball joints, worn or loose sway-bar links, separated lower control bushings that are pulling away, broken springs, leaking and weak shocks/struts, leaking power-steering lines, and noisy power-steering pumps. Hunter Engineering data suggests that 3 out of 10 vehicles require additional front-end components. These services are normally simple to identify and easy to replace and repair, so there are no comebacks once the wheel alignment has been completed properly. This is why I have been discussing this topic in such detail.

Visible Wheel Alignment Problems

- Crooked steering wheel.
- Vehicle pulls or drifts.
- Tires show abnormal wear patterns.

Non-visible Wheel Alignment Problems

- Lost fuel economy of 4% or more.
- Compromised safety.
- Rapid or increased tire wear.

Customer Awareness Tools

- Helping customers understand the color spec printout of the Hunter Engineering Quick-Check is a must.
- Use props such as Hunter Network displays.
- Wooden model car to show wheel alignment details.
- Worn tire display.
- Worn steering parts.
- Worn suspension parts.

A customer's natural response will be to decline the purchase when the salesperson lacks the necessary air of confidence. The customers can tell when the salesperson does not understand or believe in the products. Therefore, the first person you sell must be yourself.

Targeting Non-buyers

Some field-testing data:

- 50–65% of the vehicles seen at your shop may benefit from wheel alignments.
- 1/3 of these vehicles have no visible issues.
- 40% of the vehicles will have no alignment issues.
- 40% of these vehicles will have visible alignment issues.
- 20% of these vehicles will have alignment issues that are not visible.
- 95% of customers who purchase tires will invest in a wheel alignment if needed. If you utilize the previously mentioned 'Ask' or 'Close,' you will generate great results, save the

customers a great deal of money, and make them loyal customers.

The Empowering Wheel Alignment Script

Here is another wheel alignment script to practice:

"Mrs. Jones, you are having to invest in a new set of tires prematurely due to an alignment issue that is shortening the tires' lifespan.

We have invested in some amazing new technology that captures your current wheel alignment data and compares it to the manufacturer's specs. It is highlighted in green when in spec and red when out of the manufacturer's spec. The red indicates there will be future consequences."

It is not about arm-twisting the customers but empowering them, so they clearly understand the many benefits, incredible value, and consequences of inaction. These insights will lead the customer to say 'yes' and agree to proceed with the wheel alignment. These amazing printouts are stunning and help play a very significant role in terms of loyalty and customer retention.

Here are some other illustrative examples from Hunter:

Most manufacturers do not outline a maintenance schedule for wheel alignment; however, most mechanics recommend this service be completed every 2–3 years. If you hit a curb, pothole, or debris with the Hunter Engineering unmanned system, you can now pop into your favorite auto-service center and get an alignment checkup to keep the wheels aligned. If your vehicle has an off-center steering wheel, pulls to one side while driving on a straight and level road, has uneven tire wear, or does not hold the road level, you may be due for a wheel alignment service.

Benefits of a Wheel Alignment System with Steering System Reset

As vehicle manufacturers equip more vehicles with onboard driver-assist systems, such as lane centering, electronic stability control, parking assist, traction control, and more, an increasing number of manufacturers now require a steering system reset during alignment service. Therefore, it is important to have an alignment system to reset all alignment-related sensors during alignment service.

Quick Check Drive

With Hunter's unmanned alignment inspection system, Quick Check Drive, you can now accelerate your alignment business with an automated inspection.

Each Quick Check Drive is equipped with eight cameras and 32 laser sensors that scan a vehicle's tires as they drive past, eliminating operator labor and stopping the vehicle. The system can scan a vehicle every 3–5 seconds, meaning no service drive backup, making it possible to check <u>every</u> car that visits your shop.

Printouts

Hands-on HunterNet (HunterNetwork.com) provides front-shop personnel with quick, convenient access to a vast collection of vehicle-specific under-car information to help explain and sell service.

Selling Tools

- Display and view results automatically.
- Present and email inspection details digitally.
- Inform customers using photos and videos.
- Drive repair authorization and revenue to new levels.
- Sales tool results in seconds.
- Build a printed layout that is unique to your business and uses all of the available space on the printout. Select the format that has the highest impact with Print Configurations.

Eliminates Trips Around the Car

An unmanned solution means faster scans with less labor.

Captures Data with Unmatched Accuracy

Eight cameras and 32 lasers produce results with world-class precision.

Space-efficient Design

Requires 25% less bay space than other inspection units.

Automatic Alignment Check

Patented touch-less alignment angle measures total toe and individual camber.

Automatic Results Display

Automatic display of alignment results provides complete customer transparency, ideal for service drives and waiting rooms.

- Unmanned inspection is brilliant, powerful, and impactful.

Hunter Engineering Quick Check Drive and Quick Tread Edge Integration

- Independent alignment inspection and edge-wear detection.
- Measure camber, total toe, and tire tread depth on every vehicle.
- Electronic and printed results in seconds.
- **Automatic Plate Identification:** Patent Pending-automatically determines OEM specs on most vehicles and captures front and rear license plates on every vehicle.
- Optional safeguard against false damage reports, images stored online for 15 days, 90-day premium storage available.

Hunter's patented Quick Check Drive technology is the only touchless alignment check with the proven accuracy and reliability necessary to earn over 15 OEM approvals.

Used with permission from Hunter Engineering Co.

Overview

For the Shop:

- Captures every service opportunity with a streamlined process.
- Saves time and energy by eliminating duplicate entries.
- More satisfying experience for enthusiastic technicians.
- Ensures that profitable service recommendations are always presented to customers.
- Choose your integration partner.
- Maximizes revenue.
- Increases customer retention.

For the Customer:

- Present digital inspection results.
- Make a tire replacement offer for the vehicle.
- Add services to repair order.

For a More Profitable Future:

- Automate electronic multipoint inspection items.
- Capture digital photos and videos.
- Increase technical productivity.

For the Service Advisor:

- Mobile delivery of inspection results via text or email.
- Self-guided, informative service experience.

- Interactive content with photos and videos.
- Sell more services to off-site customers on the go.

As an automotive service career person, I see this technology not as a cost but rather as an investment that has an amazing effect on ROI. Consumers see the value of authorizing the repair order in the tire DNA stats. Consumers can see the value of authorizing the repair order and in the tire's DNA stats. I recommend visiting the Hunter Engineering website and looking at the ten-year breakdown of the investment pay-off. It is money in the retirement bank.

"At American Express, we view service not as a cost but as an investment in building customer relationships."

–James P. Bush (Former President of American Express Global Network and International Consumer Services)

The final step is now in your lap. Make the right call. Visit the Hunter Engineering service representative, or Google it and watch the results change right before your eyes in light of the statement by James P. Bush.

Clearly understand that third-party technology does that salesmanship for you by presenting a colorful, powerful document (seeing is believing) to the consumers. Hand it to them, and let them take it in. It is powerful, and I am confident that by sharing this powerful document, it will sell itself.

"Of course, the key is to introduce the right offers to the right customers at the right times. Not everything to everyone all the time."

–Steve Jobs

Hunter Engineering Alignment Quick Check Alignment's Financial Business Model

Growing an Additional Revenue Stream Beyond Your Wildest Dream

My journey with Hunter Engineering started when I met their great team at the SEMA Apex Auto Show in Las Vegas. The testimonial was in my last year (2009) as a service manager. A guest purchased the Hunter Engineering wheel alignment equipment. He had two-wheel alignment machines and four racks. Let us do the math to see the unbelievable potential that is too often overlooked. The purchase resulted directly from educating the consumer on the amazing benefits and incredible value it offers. Doing a wheel alignment on time extended the tire life, thus maximizing tread life, reducing the stress and fatigue on the steering components, increasing mileage, and reducing greenhouse gas byproducts. Value still motivates the consumer to buy in with the purchase. Another big factor today is the amazing drive-thru technology. Today, it is so simple, quick, and easy. All one has to do is invest in the amazing Hunter Engineering Quick Check machine.

The secret is in the math. The formula will demonstrate that it is NOT a cost but rather a great investment that quickly pays off.

The Amazing Business Model and Experience in My Last Year of Being a Service Manager in Saskatoon

In 2009, there were 4,086 wheel alignment purchases.

4,086 @ $109.99 per alignment = $449,419.14

What about all the auxiliary pieces? With front-steering components, suspension pieces, struts, leaking hoses, tires, and more, that number can easily be doubled.

The industry data suggest that 3–to 4 out of every 10 vehicles will require additional front steering and suspension components.

Back to the math.

Half of those vehicles will need additional steering components.

50% (of the original 4,086) = 2,043

1.2 units of labor for every second vehicle in the aftermarket i.e. for tie rods (loose), sway bar links (worn and loose), ball joints (loose), leaking struts or shocks (leaking), leaking or dipping power steering hose(s) at the same labor charge-out rate of $125.00 = $255,375

An additional upsell (since it is obvious) that is deemed as "required" is pointed out. Let us add in the cost of the parts - that is an average of $255,375. Let us use industry data that, at minimum, 10% of the vehicles will need new tires as well, (and these numbers are very conservative):

10% of 2,043 = 204 sets of tires at an estimated cost of $1,200 = $244,800 in additional tires sales.

Let us add up the numbers/do the math:

Wheel alignments	$449,419
Labor (additional on parts)	$255,375

Parts associated with repairs	$255,375
Tires required and sold 10%	$244,800
The total of the Opportunity	$1,204,969
Profit Projection of 25%	$310,992
Assumption (75% or above)	$233,244
Cost of Hunter Quick Check	$50,000
Return on Investment (after Cost)	$183,244
Multiplied over ten years =	$1,832,440

There are two key artificial intelligence or smart devices to invest in: Winning Big with Hunter Engineering (AI tool) and Digital Vehicle Inspection platform (AutoSevre1 is a smart tool). Artificial intelligence is not a cost; rather, it is a smart investment that yields returns above and beyond your wildest imagination. If you are not investing, you are missing the boat and a plethora of opportunities. The data clearly and boldly claims the added value of these tools has an effect equal to hiring additional technicians; it multiplies and generates great opportunities.

Let us look at this: your traffic number is 10,000 consumers on an annual basis. The average cost for a wheel alignment would be around $109.00 multiplied by 6,500 (65% failure rate) = $708,500 - the number of vehicles that require a wheel alignment. Let us be real. We will not have this percentage buy-in, so let us use a more realistic number of 20%; and take the time to walk those consumers through the amazing benefits and incredible value it represents. During my consulting time in the industry, I would ask the service manager to take me out to the tire recycling storage area and closely examine all the tires that have been replaced. By focusing on the DNA of the recycled tires, it could be seen that approximately 75% of consumers did not receive full value out of their investment in tires. Due to not having their wheel alignment checked regularly (99.9% of the auto service centers offer this service at no charge).

With today's large-sized tires, which are very expensive, the wheel alignment outside the manufacturer's spec will cause tires to wear rapidly, thus shortening the tire life. This will cause stress and fatigue on the steering components, ultimately weakening the tie rods prematurely and causing the wheel to be out of alignment, which will then cause greater fuel consumption and spew out emissions, depending on the setting. With the alignment done on time, the vehicle owner could have 4–6% more in savings, plus an extended tire life, and they will not have to pay for an expensive tie rod and the cost of installation. As you can see, a wheel alignment issue becomes a very expensive experience. In 13 months with the Hunter Engineering Quick Wheel Alignment Check, we generated 2,000 new wheel alignments despite missing out on several opportunities. That is not good. However, this artificial intelligence machine has alerted us to new revenue and legitimate opportunities. The consumer benefits from tires having an extended life, closer to the manufacturer's mileage rating recommendation.

The Quick Check alignment machine identified that 1,625 vehicles needed a wheel alignment, sold at $109.00, generating a total revenue of $177,125.00.

Here is the bonus: 50% of these vehicles need new tires, and 10% will purchase a set of tires. So, let us say 50% or half of the 1,625 vehicles will need additional steering or suspension components. Let us factor in the number of 1.2 units (labor units) at the door rate of $109.00, which is equal to $130.80, and, when multiplied by 1,625, generates an additional labor revenue of $212,550.00.

Add a similar amount for parts, and the additional revenue is $212,550.00 for under-car issues like the tie rod, the loose ball joints, the sway bar links, and the leaking front struts, simply because you had your eyes open to do a validated inspection to help the consumer with peace of mind motoring or at least make them aware so they can adjust their budget over the next months. So let us calculate the total additional new revenue that this has generated:

Financial Revenue Model of the Store in Calgary (when I served there as Service Manager): 2,500 New Wheel Alignments were purchased in 13 Months (prior year 489):

2111 additional/new wheel alignments at $109.00 generated an income of = $230,099.00 plus 489 X $109 = $53,301 for a total of $283.400.00 (based on 2500 wheel alignments).

Half =1,250 needed 1.2 additional labor @ $109.00 charge-out hourly rate = $130.80 X 813 = $136,250.00

Plus additional parts revenue (which is an industry average of 1 to 1) = $136,250.00

Grand Total of new revenue generated = $535,900.00

(This is a very achievable #)

Here is the amazing secret; this number ($535,900.00) should be times 10 years (without any additional growth) bringing the long-range revenue to the more realistic number of:

$5,359,000.00

Using a margin percentage of 30 points for profit, it generates $1,607,770.00 profit gained. A nice return on investment was generated from one area, the suspension. Wow! That is ROI and a win-win for the consumer, the business, and the cast members.

Finally, visit their website, watch, and rewatch the two powerful and brilliant videos, 'Introduction To Wheel Alignment' and 'Sell the Benefits of Alignment,' to completely educate the consumer, so they are empowered and sell themselves.

Testimonials Discussed below Are Powerful

Hunter Quick Check Inspection – last month, we did 418 alignments.

–Todd Heitz, Greenway Automotive Group – Alignment business doubled with Push Reports at Greenway

Greenway DCJR was looking for more insight into how their Hunter Engineering equipment was utilized in their service drive to help their fixed operations business. So, when Todd Heitz, Greenway's national director of fixed operations, learned about Hunter's new Push Reports, he found exactly what he was looking for! "The Greenway has been in business for a little over 20 years – starting from one store here in Orlando, F.L. – we have grown now to be 47 stores across the country in eight different states – take a hard look at how much financial opportunity is sitting back there coming across your drive every day – the alignments have been around for years – we have handed that business to a lot of the independent service providers because we didn't take the time, but now, with this tool, we can check the vehicle specs and alignment on the service drive at the time of write up which is our best opportunity while we are in front of the customer.

When we first started with the inspection equipment, we were doing 110–120 alignments per month – now we have a report that comes out at noon and 8:00 p.m. every single day – there is no 'Are they using it or are they not?' After a week's worth of piloting this and not telling them, I called him and said, 'Hey, how many cars do you think you are checking a day?' I tried to tell him around 60–65, and he said you did 30. And the phone went silent. He didn't argue with me – he didn't challenge me. It was kind of a slap in the face – you take those things one of two ways – either a negative and put your head down, or you can take it as a challenge.

On Wednesday, the very next day, we inspected 92 vehicles. On Thursday, we inspected 98 – we went from averaging 180–200 a month to last month where we did 418 to the tune of $30,000 in gross – it was exciting for me when we went from $12–$15,000 a month, just a couple of months ago to $30,000 overnight because of the Push Reports. It is about the 100% buy-in, by 100% of the team, 100% of the time. Learn this lesson: this is for the consumer, and let us be 100% committed to them.

Not only is it paying for itself, but now, the demand is there for more equipment that will pay for itself in a matter of 3–4 months – by doing one thing – and That is implementing, following up, looking at a report, and holding people accountable to one process."

After Quick Check – 500 alignment checks, 180–200 alignments, $12–$15K gross profits

With Push Reports – 2,000 alignment checks, 410 alignments, $30K gross profits

"Hunter Quick Check Inspection – this machine pays for itself in months, not years."

–Terry West, Eddy's Toyota – Chief Operations Officer for Eddy's Group – Toyota in Wichita, Kansas

Seven dealerships installed Quick Check Drive automated alignment inspection systems in their service drives and saw an immediate return on investment, increasing their alignment sales by 300%!

"Bringing hours into the shop – bringing customers into the shop – is my priority – so, anytime there is new technology out there, I have to entertain that because it is all about my employees.

"Sales rep for Hunter, Bruce Anderson, came into my office – my relationship with Bruce is funny – I used to kick him out of my office all the time – one day, he came in and said – I need one minute of your time – he put an iPad in front of me and showed me the quick check drive, and it was love at first sight, and when I saw this piece of equipment – I knew I could build customer retention with it – I could offer the customer something that nobody else had – it was a no-brainer to put it in all the stores, plus this machine paid for itself in months and not years.

"When we got the Quick Check Drive, we got billboards, and free alignment checks went on those billboards right away – when the customer pulls in, the first thing it does is, take 40 pictures of the vehicle – it protects the customer and protects us against body damage claims, which, at Toyota, typically runs at $6,000 and $8,000 a month – the flight board and the 85" monitor was a big deal to me because every time they pull in, they were going to look at the board and see their car is still in alignment. Since we put in the Quick Check Drive, our alignment sales went up 300%, which is amazing. In February, we sold 38 alignments total for the entire month. After getting Quick Check Drive, we sold 161 alignments. In subsequent months, I would not be surprised to see us hit the 300-plus alignments per month with our equipment.

"I did the math; 30 alignments a day will generate just under one million dollars in retail alignment sales in 12 months. I saw that this alignment check had so much potential, and I saw that there was no way my alignment machines were going to keep up, so we purchased two Hunter Alignment Machines in conjunction with the Quick Check Drive, knowing that the volume was going to exceed our capabilities. Hunter equipment is quality and efficient, so when you start bringing equipment in, it makes everybody's job easier and faster, and it is a win-win. Alignment sales increased by 300%, and body damage claims decreased by 90%."

#wechoosehunter – *"They do not expect that kind of technology at a tire store."*

–Mark Rhodes, Plaza Tire Service, President – Cape Drone, Missouri

"We own and operate 67 retail tire stores. Our original thought process was to make sure that we did every vehicle some sort of alignment check – with all our quick check machines, it added gross profit – and revenue, and it protects our core business, which is the sale of tires. To make sure that the tires that we put on work correctly and last longer. Right now, we are currently going to put unmanned systems in all our new locations – our goal is to have them in every location. Other benefits of the unmanned system – are the cameras; the way it is set up, it naturally captures the license plate number – you catch if there is a hub cap missing or any kind of body damage –now and again, you get customers who question whether it was that way when it came in, so now you have proof how the vehicle looked when it came in. With all our quick check machines, we have flight boards – we always position the flight boards in a spot where the customer and our counter people can see them, so they can reference the customer's car when it comes across the flight board and, in our world, speed is everything. The faster we can get it in front of the customer, the faster we can get the job done, making more sales. Consumers are always wowed by it because they do not expect that type of technology in a tire store, and when you do get the printout, or see the flight board, a picture is worth a thousand words – it shows the health of their car in one image. We dedicate ourselves to having hawk-eye machines and doing our alignments in all our 67 locations. For the safety systems that we can upgrade with them, we use the Hunter Net to follow up with some stores on push reports and monitor their sales on different key elements – alignments, balancing, and quick checks. A great benefit is to keep us in touch with the stores daily – we are believers in the quick check systems – we know that we get every vehicle inspected, and we are going to sell more products and have a better retention rate with our customers – also more efficiently and faster, as speed is the main thing we look at in servicing our customers."

The Takeaway

The steering and suspension area has the most common failure rates than any other vehicle area and is the most lucrative. Hunter Engineering Quick Check Alignment machine identifies whether the alignment is in the manufacturer's spec. It also captures the tire tread groove depth and provides an additional valuable area: the tires. Three out of every ten vehicles need or require tires. The secret is that the first service provider to bring it to the consumer's attention will win the lottery. Over time, the numbers add up considerably, which is another bonus. The other secret is that consumers, in a great percentage of cases, will purchase all their preventative maintenance services from where they bought the tires.

Just the fact that you have invested in this brilliant AI will compel consumers to come back to your service and repair facility. This provides the consumer with the comfort of third-party neutral evaluation along with amazing Disney-like customer service. These experiences will lead to numerous positive reviews that will attract consumers, further increasing the traffic at your doors.

The financial business model will yield an amazing look at the true potential and growth that will be very rewarding.

Without question, I strongly recommend digesting this information. Go to Hunter's website and watch the amazing videos until such a time when it is completely internalized within you. This will pay extremely well, and you will see growth as a result of more knowledge and greater confidence. The mind is powerful and useful IF it absorbs the right information. I encourage you to become more than you ever expected. Become a superstar. Execute this chapter, and you will rock!

NOTES

Chapter 9

The Million Dollar Opportunity

"Vision is the gift to see what others only dream."

–Byrd Baggett

The Power of Educating Versus Selling

What is in It for Me, (WIIFM)- The Consumer

Can I Show You the Money?

A lot of consumers do not understand the preventative maintenance schedule. You have to print out this empowering document and hand it to them. Seeing it for themselves makes the services more believable, as long as they have already been educated on the amazing benefits and value. Real winners will put in the time and hard work to master delivering the scripts discussed in this chapter, while pretenders will read them once or twice, attempt to deliver them, and fall flat on their faces. When you are not committed, your results will be half-baked.

When I'd ask these half-committed advisors, *"How did it go?"* Their response would be, *"The customers were not interested."* I would then approach the clients and advise them, confidently, that they should do the preventative maintenance since it was past the manufacturer's recommended interval schedule. I would also inform them that the transmission fluid was very dark and had a burnt odor. Then the customer would reconsider.

When you, as an advisor, deliver the script with confidence by educating clients, you feel good because you have empowered the consumer. Then you become a superstar because you successfully created that magical Disney moment for your customer.

This is why a structured process is so important and needs to be followed. The appropriate language must be consistently delivered. You cannot wing it or fake it. Your closing percentage will only go up when you have mastered the scripts. Only <u>Perfect</u> practice makes <u>Perfect</u>; that is the secret.

This approach eliminates manipulation and pressure, so the customer is no longer making a grudge purchase. The carefully executed process reassures them, so they do not feel as though they have been given the hard sell.

The Perfect Art of Delivering Amazing Customer Service is about communication. A case in point is to watch the client's body language while sharing the benefits and values of the needed preventative maintenance schedule. You will see them nod their heads, which means you have connected with them. Most often, they will interrupt you and ask for the price and the time it takes to execute the service. The buy-in then becomes easy, as the consumer sees it as an investment on account of being empowered.

In my own vehicle ownership experience, I have never had to replace any significant components like an engine, transmission, differential, transfer case, power steering pump, radiator, front-end, steering, or suspension parts. I have invested in preventative maintenance, as endorsed by all vehicle manufacturers. This includes tire manufacturers. I recognized that I could retain the full-cycle value of my tires by watching their DNA, which today's technologies permit. Checking tire pressure regularly allows owners to obtain the complete full-cycle value of the investment. You do a tremendous favor to consumers by communicating these empowering things to them. The secret is to involve and engage them in the whole ownership and maintenance process, and they will stay with you.

The Unbelievable Win

Here is a powerful idea: you, as a dealer, can, in many cases, grow your ROI by double digits. I have experienced this, as did my dealer and the staff. But most of all, the consumers were the big winners, simply because of all the money they saved.

The Winning Formula That Drives Preventative Maintenance

Remember, the secret is to follow structured processes and establish the consumer's real needs and wants. Your job is about educating, walking the customer to their vehicle, and having the technician demonstrate the case for recommended service. Show-and-tell actively involves them, and they get it right away. When handled right, this process allows the customers to sell themselves. The opportunity for selling preventative maintenance is unlimited.

However, to reach a 70% closing rate, you have to create great value. When the service manager holds the entire team accountable for their actions, You will be amazed at the achievements they make. Every preventative maintenance service recommended by the manufacturer is in the owner's manual. Print it out and hand it to the customer. This process prevents costly repairs. Google specialty shops like those servicing automatic transmissions, and you will be shocked at the number of businesses that are winning big; You will see that you have lagged simply because you failed to change your sales culture. By not doing it, you cheat the business owner, and the tech in the shop, and you cost the consumer major dollars. Is this YOU? If so, you need to start learning the scripts for each preventative maintenance service outlined below. As I indicated, you must memorize them to win over customers. Their gratitude, followed by the technicians' and the owners', will follow. This is an honorable thing. Educating consumers on the benefits and values is one of the best retention tools in the marketplace.

Would You Board a Plane That is Never Had Preventative Maintenance?

Advisors will reflexively attempt to sell maintenance based on price. It does not work very often. Without providing benefits and value, they resort to pushy sales tactics and turn the client off. You cannot push the envelope that hard. Customer churn will then take place. You need to look further ahead than the point of sale and adopt a different cultural approach; otherwise, you will end up pushing your clients right into the arms of your competitors. Have that accountability meeting and discuss it with your cast members. Make sure your team does not pass over the business because they assume customers cannot afford it. In truth, the customers cannot afford it if they have to return and pay for something much more expensive that could have been prevented. As a service manager, you have to coach and mentor your team members. I learned that if you do this often enough, advisors will realize the level of work and practice they must put in if they want to reap the rewards. A service advisor must be prepared to be schooled – to become disciplined in knowing the benefits and values of preventative maintenance to be successful. You cannot fake it. You must have the facts at hand to answer each question and overcome each objection. You have to be believable as knowledge is power.

What Does Preventative Maintenance Do?

Preventative maintenance lowers the cost of operating a vehicle, increases its resale value, and saves consumers a lot of green stuff in their wallets. It also plays one of the fundamental roles in the automotive service business that, when offered, results in customer retention. This is because by simply checking the vehicle's mileage, the service interval schedule, or the condition of fluids, the tell-tale signs can lead customers to save big by spending only pennies per mile. Preventative maintenance is so important that all manufacturers have deliberately printed out the required and recommended service in the mileage interval schedules in their owner's manuals. They invariably state that damages or failures due to the lack of proper maintenance or neglect are not covered under their warranties

In *"Eight Keys to Selling Auto Service,"* Bob Cooper discusses some important ways to promote and lock in any business opportunity. First, he suggests the staff keep the right tools at hand. He says that since he firmly believes in the fact that people believe what they see, it is a smart tactic to involve them visually during inspections and documentation. For this, third-party documentation serves as a credible source, which includes, but is not limited to, manuals, service records, printouts of the company's recommendations, brochures, repair orders, etc. Second, he suggests that when you are calling a customer to inform them about the diagnosis, make sure to start from the "good" aspect. This sets up the tone of the conversation, and the customer feels more at ease since you haven't blurted out all the expenses they will have to bear. This will also allow you to calmly convince them to avail of your services, and it will be easier for them to believe you. A third important thing to keep in mind is to present an assumptive close. Tell them that you need their approval, and You will start right away with the service; refrain from asking questions they might say no to. Be sure to make your customers feel that they have no reason to reject your service.

Benefits and Value Service Scripts

1. Brake Fluid

a) Brake Fluid Service

According to industry standards, brake fluid should be changed every two years or approximately every 48,000 km. It is the service provider's responsibility to always check the brake fluid history and ask when it was last changed. If a brake fluid test is a failure after only one year, chances are, the technician may not have adequately flushed all the old, contaminated fluid long enough to remove the nasty elements. A brake fluid test strip, such as Phoenix Systems' FASCAR-rated strips, is a great show-and-tell that should be used at all times, as it provides third-party verification. One can see the results within 60 seconds, offering repeatable proof of copper levels in the fluid.

Make sure to show the client the outcome, even if the test has positive results. Copper serves as the most accurate measure of depleted corrosion inhibitors, so this verifiable evidence helps build trust with the vehicle owner. Put the test strip in a small plastic bag and show it to the customer alongside a printout that explains the test results. This creates instant credibility.

Brakebleeder.com discusses the use of Phoenix Systems' Brake Strip process, which indicates the necessity of a system flush: The Motorist Assurance Program (MAP) has established copper as its recommended standard for testing brake fluid to determine when brake fluid replacement is required.

Do You See Purple? If so, it may be time to change your brake fluid and extend the life of your brake system.

Once the strip is dipped in brake fluid, it begins the copper measurement reaction – changing the color from white to purple in direct proportion to the copper level. Compare the strip to the copper-corrosion color scale, and in as little as sixty seconds, you have reliable proof of whether or not the brake fluid meets the recommended guidelines.

Why conduct a test? Just like engine oil, coolant, and transmission fluid, brake fluid "wears" over time. This leaves the brake system vulnerable to corrosion, which can damage the Anti-lock brake system (ABS) and metal components.

If you see purple, it may be time to change your brake fluid and extend the life of your system.

In his March 18, 2010, article for the *Globe & Mail,* Richard Russell commented on the science of brake fluid:

"Brake fluid is highly susceptible to absorbing moisture. As this happens, it changes the very nature of the brake fluid, including the boiling point.

The hydraulic brake system is indeed sealed, but moisture can be absorbed through the seals in any system. Over time, this moisture can cause corrosion in the critical and very expensive-to-replace ABS components.

But it is the change in boiling point that is critical. The minimum boiling point of brake fluid, depending on the SAE grade, is in the range of 401 to 446°F. This is necessary because of the tremendous heat created when the pads clamp on the disc or press against a rotating drum when slowing the vehicle.

If the brake fluid reaches the boiling point, vapor bubbles are created. Brake fluid is meant to transfer pressure to the pads, pushing them against the rotors or drums. If there are tiny bubbles in the system, they are compressed when you press on the brakes, and this compression reduces the force transmitted to the brakes.

It takes only a tiny amount of moisture to bring the boiling point below the recommended minimum, and when you need maximum braking in an emergency, performance would be reduced."

A great challenge for service advisors is to explain to vehicle owners why, for safety reasons, changing the brake fluid is required. In his November 1, 2011, article for *Auto Service World,* Tom Venetis observed:

"Most drivers know that not changing your motor oil or coolant regularly will not kill you; it will just hit your pocketbook very hard as contaminates build up and damage critical systems in an engine. The problem is that not changing brake fluid regularly will not only be costly, it could very well cause the driver to have an accident. Changing brake fluid regularly is not just a maintenance issue but a safety one as well.

What is unique about these fluids is that they are hygroscopic. This means that they can mix with water and still perform their function in the brake system. Silicone-based fluids, referred to as DOT 5, are non-hygroscopic, so they will not absorb or mix with water.

Water is the enemy. Take the issue of moisture. You cannot avoid it. It is all around us, from rain to the moisture that is in the air. Ethylene Glycol-based brake fluid will, over time, absorb moisture from the surrounding air. Brake fluid is made to have a high boiling point to withstand the high heat produced when the vehicle brakes. When new and without any water in the mix, brake fluid will boil at about 260°C. When moisture gets into the system, that boiling point drops and can drop to a level close to that of ordinary water.

When this happens, the brake system is compromised.

Now, it has to be admitted that old brake fluid will work well for most normal driving conditions. In badly deteriorated brake fluid, the driver may discover that when applying the brakes, the vehicle simply does not stop."

Once again, the reason most service advisors are unsuccessful in selling preventative maintenance services is that they do not understand how the systems function. Thus, the sale is lost, and the customer has zero confidence in you and your service.

b) The Empowering Brake Flush Service Script

"Mrs. Smith, the technician tested your vehicle's brake fluid with an industry test strip, which has strongly indicated a high level of copper, which is created by the absorption of moisture. This reduces the boiling point, which can cause the brake pedal to go to the floor. Brake fluid is hygroscopic, which means it absorbs moisture from rain and air and causes it to become contaminated."

(Show the brake strip and have the advisor read the brake strip info card)

"Our technicians will flush and remove all the contaminated, worn-out brake fluid and refill the system with upgraded fluid.

"Mrs. Smith, I am sure you see the benefits of having enhanced braking ability and the great value in keeping your brake system safe in an emergency when the brake pedal needs to be held down for several seconds to avoid accidents. The newly updated brake fluid will give you that enhanced stopping ability, giving you peace of mind and protecting yourself and your family, as well as eliminating the expense of a potentially damaged ABS. The cost is $119.00, and

we can have it completed within thirty minutes. Does this work for you?"

Then you can say,

"How would you like us to proceed with keeping your vehicle safe and in roadworthy condition?"

You must know the background information in the event the consumer asks a related question. When you have memorized the script and understood the material, the knowledge gives you the confidence to effectively emphasize the benefits and great, solid value every preventative maintenance offers.

The automotive industry needs passionate people who will challenge themselves. You are the only one able to advance your career to the level of supervisor or manager. To earn more, you must commit to knowing more.

2. Coolant

a) Coolant Flush Service

You should always ask the customer if their vehicle has ever had a coolant flush service. More importantly, the service advisor must get into the habit of checking the manufacturer's recommended interval service schedule and printing it out to show the customer. Be professional. The maximum longevity of coolant is now about four to five years, after which it loses its effectiveness, as Patrice Banks observes in "What is a Coolant Flush and Does My Car Need It?"

Coolant needs to be flushed because it breaks down over the years and then loses the ability to serve its purpose of maintaining the optimum temperature of the engine and preventing corrosion. Dirt and dust particles floating inside the coolant can clog your radiator or heater core.

In their "Standard Test Method for Reserve Alkalinity of Engine Coolants and Anti-rusts," ASTM International provides the science behind coolant quality as it relates to proper engine function:

"Reserve alkalinity is the number of milliliters, to the nearest 0.1 mL of 0.100 N hydrochloric acid (HCl) required for the titration to a pH of 5.5 of a 10-mL sample of an undiluted, unused coolant, anti-rust, or coolant additive, and unused or used solutions thereof."

What this means is that broken-down coolant will become acidic and, over time, cause heater cores and the radiator to leak. The failure to follow the manufacturer's recommended interval service schedule will be very hard on the pocketbook. ASTM continues:

"Reserve alkalinity is a term applied to engine coolants and anti-rusts to indicate the number of alkaline components present in the product. It is frequently used for quality control during production, and values are often listed in specifications. When applied to used solutions, reserve alkalinity gives an approximate indication of the amount of remaining alkaline components. Unfortunately, the term is sometimes misused in that its numerical value is said to be directly related to coolant quality; the higher the number, the better the coolant."

Many of these concerns can be diagnosed efficiently by conducting a coolant strip test. Another purpose is to check the product's boiling and freezing points. A very low freezing point can quickly damage the coolant system's components. In the 'How Important is a Coolant

Flush?' September 2, 2016, article on ricksautoservice.org, several points are offered, arguing for the value of this service.

Why have a properly maintained cooling system in the winter:

- Freeze protection.
- Continued protection against overheating.
- Reduced thermal stress by having uniform temperatures around your engine and radiator.
- Improved cabin heater efficiency.
- There is a science behind a coolant system flush, and it is valuable for professionals to be aware of it.

Techmax.ca elaborates on the antifreeze-water balance question in "What is a Cooling System Service?"

"The proper mix is determined by checking the coolant level; -35 degrees equals 50/50. The problem comes when the pH of water is 7.0 to 7.2, and the antifreeze pH is 10.5 right out of the gallon. A 50/50 mix of water and antifreeze would have a pH factor of 8.75. This level is too acidic for today's cooling systems. The recommended pH level should be between 9.8 and 10.5; this level greatly reduces the acid content that, together with the electrochemical reaction of dissimilar materials, causes electrochemical degradation.

To correct the above condition, you need to power flush your cooling system by continuously forcing the coolant, under pressure, through the engine, radiator, and heater core in both directions at different times. Once this is done, antifreeze or water is added to the system while circulating to bring it to the desired temperature throughout the system evenly. We then add a pH concentrate while still circulating the coolant evenly to reach a pH level of 10.5 throughout the system. We stop at 10.5 pH because, over time, as the hot coolant flows through the system, it will slowly become more acidic, as described above. The coolant should stay within the safe range of 9.8 to 10.5 pH level for about 2 years or 30,000 miles. We also conduct a pressure test on the system for leaks, clean the recovery bottle, and test the radiator cap to see if it holds the proper pressure."

To check the pH reserve alkalinity and boiling and freezing points, the auto service industry has developed a strip test that can effectively communicate the benefits and values of this data, which independently establishes integrity and trust. Likewise, the preventative maintenance interval schedules in owner's manuals also play vital roles in prudent vehicle ownership. The industry can attest that a failure to perform multi-point inspections can result in numerous issues that otherwise would not have been caught by the technicians: clogged radiators and cracked hoses causing overheated engines, leading to expensive engine damage; cracked water pumps that leak acid, caused by a failure to change the coolant, damaging the heater core, and AC systems that cease to function. Not to mention all the secondary consequences for the owner of the vehicle, such as missing important meetings, the need for tow trucks, and spending money on hotels and car rentals.

Servicing and replacing the coolant will extend the life of the hoses, water pump, heater core, thermostat radiator, and, in some cases, the engine if it becomes overheated. The radiator is responsible for cooling the transmission fluid, and the acid from degraded coolant will often corrode its separate cooling tank and leak coolant into the transmission.

b) The Empowering Coolant Flush Script

"This service will help prevent overheating, and the special lubricants in the new coolant will help prevent premature water pump failure, giving you peace of mind for the next 60,000 km."

"Mr. Jones, we have checked the manufacturer's coolant service interval, which requires that the coolant system be flushed every X km. We have also performed an industry coolant test using this strip which indicates a high level of pH, so the boiling and freezing point tests have failed. In other words, your vehicle's coolant has surpassed its life cycle and requires a flush and service. Have you ever serviced or changed the coolant?"

And the customer says, "Never," so then continue with

"We recommend you follow the manufacturer's interval service schedule to eliminate costly repairs to the heater core and/or radiator, which are common. The tech has carefully checked the hoses and water pump for leaks, and we are glad to report that, at this time, the only required work is the coolant flush and service. The benefits are numerous and have great value as they reduce the need to replace expensive coolant system parts."

"The benefits are better efficiency and improved air conditioner performance to optimize the vehicle's climate control features. It will eliminate breakdowns due to overheating, and provide longer life for the engine and all related components like the radiator and heater core. Preventative maintenance service will provide trouble-

free, peace-of-mind driving. The cost of the complete service is only $XXX.XX and the technician can complete it in the next hour."

"Mr. Jones, I am sure you see the benefits and value of this vital service which the manufacturer indicates should be done at your vehicle's current mileage. We can complete it in the next forty-five minutes. Does this work for you?"

"How would you like us to proceed with protecting your vehicle and reducing expensive repairs?"

In all cases, be prepared to overcome objections such as time or cost. If time is the issue, offer a shuttle or ride. If it is cost, advise the consumer that you or the manager have done a competitive market shop analysis, and the price is a great value. You may also mention that you have financing available if necessary.

3. Transmission

a) Transmission Fluid Service

Transmissions operate at very hot temperatures, which, over time, break down the transmission fluid, impairing its ability to lubricate the many moving parts. Extreme heat – especially after the vehicle has been pulling a trailer – causes the fluid to take on a gummy, varnish-like quality with small particles floating within it. At the bottom of the transmission oil pan is a magnet that draws out tiny particles, which are the cause of damage.

I am a big believer that the transmission filter should be replaced during the transmission service, though some manufacturers build non-serviceable transmissions with no pans. However, just as every manufacturer has an engine oil filter and strongly recommends it be replaced during the engine oil change, the transmission filter should be replaced during a transmission service.

Remember that contaminated fluid shortens the transmission lifespan, whereas fresh fluid extends it. As with other services, taking the time to print off the OEM recommended service interval schedule shows you have the customer's best interests in mind and gives you instant credibility. Use a BG Dab-a-lube tray to demonstrate the contrast between the new fluid and the old, broken-down fluid.

At any given time, you can show the condition of the old fluid versus the new fluid, and the sales process will become much easier. Having laid this groundwork, below is a model to follow that will ease the conversation with the client.

b) The Empowering Transmission Flush Service Script

"Mr. Smith, your transmission fluid mileage has gone beyond the manufacturer's interval service schedule recommendation. When the technician inspected the fluid, it was degraded to the point where it could not protect the transmission's many moving parts. The tech has used a Dab-a-lube tray to provide you with a comparison between the new and the broken-down fluid."

"The reason you see so many transmission specialty shops is that so many service shops fail to inspect the vital transmission fluids, or they do not communicate the real benefits and solid value that manufacturers deem necessary. The failure to change this fluid promptly could become very expensive. Following the manufacturer's

guidelines will cost less than 10% of what it would be to repair or rebuild the unit."

"Mr. Smith, your transmission fluid is very dark and has a burnt odor. The tech's road test indicated it is shifting hard. New fluid will provide cooler, more efficient operation and will extend the transmission's life by protecting the internal and external lip seals. So, the shifting response and performance will be better and smoother. This vital service follows the manufacturer's recommendation and will protect the expensive investment in your vehicle, which is still in good condition."

"Mr. Smith, at this point, you have exceeded the service interval mileage and are living on borrowed time. Do you see the benefits and great value in completing this service now? With your authorization, we will install a new filter and replace all the fluid, then do a complete road test to make sure your vehicle will perform well for a long time to come. The cost is $249.99, and we can have you back on the road within a short time. I just need your OK here."

Review these ideas until you can quote them by memory. Say it to the person in the mirror and work at it until you have nailed it. Ask the service manager to role-play this process with you to improve your confidence. It has worked thousands of times before. There is only one person who can hold you back from becoming a superstar, and that is you!

4. Drive Line

a) Drive Line Service

Again, look at the manufacturer's recommended service schedule, undo the transmission fill plug, and check inside the casing with your finger for a quick estimate of its condition. Put the contents into a Dab-a-lube tray. In most cases, you will be amazed at how pitch black the fluid is, not to mention the oil seeping from the axle seals. Share the findings with the customer using the Dab-a-lube tray. This service naturally includes the rear differential, the front differential, and the transfer case if the vehicle has an all-wheel or 4-wheel drive system. This is one of the most overlooked services in the industry, but the North American data indicates that driveline service is in the top five in need of work. I believe this service has great potential because most shops fail to follow the proper processes, despite being quick and functionally efficient with today's equipment.

One should focus on the process. To be successful, you have to be obsessed with it. That means grading yourself; if you are not closing at an 85% rate in the preventative maintenance area, you need to revisit, re-tool, re-equip, and have staff attend a refresher course. The backbone of a quality service experience is built on a design similar to a factory setting, where perfect processes are repeatable and executed consistently.

b) The Empowering Drive Line Service Script

"Mrs. Jones, as part of the fluid maintenance check, the tech found your vehicle's differential fluids are past due. The sample he found shows the fluid is worn out and requires replacement. It could be upgraded to a synthetic lubricant with new technology that extends the drivetrain's life, thus increasing the longevity of the driveline – which takes a beating. This will provide a quieter operation and better performance and prevent any of the 'slip/pop' noises heard in limited-slip differentials."

"The transfer case fluid is in the same condition. This system does the same type of heavy-duty work and requires a flush and replacement with synthetic fluid. The cost of synthetic is a few dimes more, but with your vehicle's mileage and the old fluid's condition, I recommend this upgrade to better protect the transfer case and both differentials. Mrs. Jones, the true value is in greatly extending the life of your vehicle. This is a worthwhile investment. With your authorization, we can have these services completed in the next hour. I see you nodded several times as I shared this information. The cost is $XXX.XX, which amounts to pennies over the next ten years. Can I provide a shuttle ride and call you once we have completed the servicing, road test, and rechecked our guaranteed work?"

5. Power Steering

a) Power Steering Service

This system also requires checking the manufacturer's interval schedule service and vehicle history. This is another service where the Dab-a-lube should be shown to the customer to provide a better level of comfort and confidence.

As identified in a multi-point inspection, the power steering fluid will need to be checked against the current mileage and the manufacturer's recommended service interval schedule. Printing this information is paramount. When combined with the Dab-a-lube results, the information will strengthen the process you are about to deliver.

b) The Empowering Power Steering Service Script

During the status call, one should ask the customer when the preventative maintenance was last done (if ever).

"The benefit of flushing and servicing the power steering will alleviate steering pump squeal and correct noisy, erratic steering. The new fluid will extend the power steering pump's life. In cold weather, the old, sludgy fluid does not flow very easily and thus, forces it at high RPMs, causing weak power steering hoses to leak or blow out. Flushing the power steering system with cleaning agents and using a synthetic fluid will extend its life."

6. Fuel Induction

a) Fuel Induction Service

Customers read the advisor's confidence, (or lack thereof), in their faces. And this confidence sells. More importantly, it creates an appetite to buy because it connects the buyer to the message of benefits and value. The more effective and meaningful the language used is, the more amazing the results will be. Consumers are buying something rather than being sold. Once again, to be effective, before closing a fuel induction service sale, print out the recommended service interval schedule and mileage and show it to the client.

b) The Empowering Fuel Induction Script

"Mrs. Jones, you made an appointment based on your vehicle's drivability and performance concerns. After the tech completed the road test and upon visual inspection, he observed contamination build-up in the throttle body."

"Based on the manufacturer's fuel induction system interval maintenance, your vehicle has surpassed the mileage recommendation. This is often a forgotten preventative service. The fuel and air induction service use specially formulated chemicals that will clean the whole system and remove the build-up of deposits that, over time, require a thorough restoration."

"The benefits are that it revives diminished power, improves fuel economy, and restores performance to original levels."

"Mrs. Jones, I am confident You will see the true value and savings. This service investment will pay you back with improved performance and better fuel economy. The cost is $149.99, and the tech can complete it within the hour. Does this work for you?"

A Formula to Analyze Your Shop Mix of Preventative Maintenance

The need for an oil change should be checked on every visit. Overfilled oil leads to very high engine failure rates. When under the fill mark, the oil will be broken down badly. If the mileage is past the posted sticker, the failure rate (and opportunity) is 24%. Oil change revenue divided by total revenue equals the percentage of oil changes. Having a high sell-through rate of the manufacturer's preventative maintenance is essential since it is designed to save customers money when performed at the recommended intervals. Providing a menu of these services helps consumers understand their importance.

Your Goal

Maintenance revenue should be at least 50% of your repair orders. Maintenance penetration is an obvious opportunity to dramatically eliminate and reduce overall ownership operation costs. Preventative maintenance costs, in contrast to repair costs, are very low.

Maintenance is where the real opportunity lies for both consumers and businesses. It drives growth and profitability and is a great client retention and loyalty tool.

- Repair revenue divided by total revenue equals the percentage of repairs.
- Maintenance revenue divided by total revenue equals the percentage of maintenance.

Increase Shop Efficiency

Maintenance adds value, which increases your shop's efficiency (hours flagged divided by hours worked). Maintenance can frequently be completed much quicker than in the actual time allotted.

Decrease One-line Labor Repair Orders

A low percentage of one-line ROs directly reflects a failure to focus on solid processes such as completing multi-point vehicle inspections. This is another argument for investing in Digital Vehicle Inspection (DVI) platforms; techs who otherwise cherry-pick from a laundry list will inevitably skip that task by initially viewing it as more difficult or more time-consuming.

Another great opportunity that is often forgotten about is following up on declined repairs and services. Repairs that are required whereby they no longer meet the industry standard or have passed their life cycle, showing signs of cracking, bending, rusting, and are worn-out, should be recommended for repair since these components have reached the end of their life cycles. The failure to inform will lead to more damages and greater costs. Slow it down, and have an informative conversation. If you do not do it, someone else (your competitor) will benefit from you short-cutting the conversation or not providing enough insight. A seasoned service advisor should work at overcoming these objections. If it is a maintenance item that is based on the manufacturer's interval schedule, you should print it out, in all cases, and explain thoroughly. The power of print documents is too often overlooked. You should also check the history for the last service and then ask when maintenance service "X" was last done. Then there is the seasonal maintenance service (in the fall, making sure the coolant system meets the industry standard); thus, preventing future repairs. The lower radiator hose could fail, or coolant loss could lead to catastrophic overheating and thermostat damage.

The air conditioning system should be checked in the spring for visible evidence of leaks which often show signs of wear. Check and replace air and cabin filters to provide passengers comfort during warmer weather. Many vehicles are neglected by the owner as they avoid that timely discussion that is started by a thorough digital vehicle inspection (DVI) whereby items cannot be skipped.

The maintenance inspection information/findings should be shared as a recommendation, where the consumer is given a "show and tell" and then further shares rather than telling; this is a much softer approach to use. Consumers often do not relate to these maintenance services, so it is your responsibility to educate them on the amazing benefits and incredible value. So, take the time to inform them; You will be surprised how many of them will just ask and inquire when it can be done. If the consumer's body language appears to be in doubt, share the consequences of not doing the service. Again, educating them about it plays a big factor.

Consumers often raise questions, and, too often, the objections are not real, so it boils down to a specific piece of information that is not shared in the conversation that concerns them. In this event, circle back and question them about why not now. Attempt to find out what the issue is. Be a little bolder; the fact is the consumers want more insight and information. Unfortunately, often the service advisors lack product knowledge. Heaven forbid they lack technical skills or have an attitude issue, causing the consumers to look for the exit door.

Two things that I want to emphasize here are, first, have quick financial apps that provide a 10-minute response time. Second, the telephone must be answered no later than the third ring. Letting it ring 5 to 8 times reflects badly on the standard of care.

Review All Job Functions

An audit should be conducted whereby every tech's job code time provides a full, fair margin. The shop labor charge-out per Hourly rate is $125.00, and the job code for a wheel alignment is one hour for the tech or unit. In addition, the price (be it door rate or the actual competitive price) may vary somewhat, so you will want to be noticeably competitive on the menu's service prices, such as for a wheel alignment.

Use New Technology

The use of new technology, such as DVI platforms on 100% of vehicles, 100% of the time, is not a cost but an investment and is not different from stocking more inventory. Acquiring Hunter Engineering's Quick-Check, with wheel alignment systems that require no heads placed on tires, can rachet up a shop's wheel alignment numbers. The amazing data, that the multitude of sensors provide, sells consumers outright, and the color print-outs can be extremely convincing. Focusing on those benefits and solid value is paramount. Use menus and MPIs *effectively.* AutoServ1 is a digital vehicle mechanical inspection platform that empowers and educates the consumer to see what is good and what is needed in real time.

Learning how to become an effective closer means learning to "Ask." A leader needs to be a great coach and mentor and then continue to invest in their team members but, at the same time, also hold them accountable to take the business to new heights and drive sales year after year. Advisors have to work at this, focus on three rock-solid points of benefits and values for each service, and deliver them in a relaxed manner. A big part of this process is understanding *Upselling* and *Cross-Selling.* These concepts are often used interchangeably, but there is a meaningful difference between the two.

Upselling is when you encourage your customers to purchase a more expensive part in the same product line or augment the original purchase with additional features. A benefit for the client would be an extended warranty, such as certain companies provide, for an additional twenty-four months for $10.00 extra. *Cross-selling* is recommending a product or service that complements an existing purchase but from a different category. If a client's vehicle has a leaking water pump, cross-selling provides an opportunity to examine its coolant pH readings or water hose or radiator for signs of deterioration. As with upselling, cross-selling can benefit consumers by preventing future repairs; the lower radiator hose could fail, or coolant loss could lead to catastrophic overheating and thermostat damage. When it comes down to "preventative maintenance" the manufacturers have clearly outlined it in the owner's manual. This reduces costly repairs and, in many cases, eliminates them almost indefinitely, thus extending the life cycle and saving a great deal of money while the owner enjoys the pleasure of great vehicle performance. Too often, we fail our customers; your role is much like a doctor who shares and recommends what one needs to have to live their best life.

Here is the best takeaway secret: tracing the cast member's performance. Customer service is the most powerful and impactful tool to drive this business, as a matter of fact, all businesses. Therefore, I would reward the cast members more on this criterion than on any other; this must be the "golden standard" and the benchmark. That is how important customer service is; it is about excellence, making it a memorable event to celebrate the real "value" that customers greatly appreciate.

The secret is tracking each cast member's closing percentage, which should be in the 60 % range, and yes, it may vary. Cast members must have these benefits and values nailed down to 100%. It is about engaging mental memory muscles so you can commit to 100%, so the scripts flow and roll off of your tongue flawlessly. As a service manager, you need to inform new hires that this is a must-have. And that once they communicate this flawlessly, they will become a rock-star. Therefore, tracking is another must-have; if someone struggles with it, the service manager must help them out. Failure comes when service advisors are unable to engage 100% of the time with 100% of the consumers.

Jamie Cuthbert from AutoServe1 provides a profound guideline for "The Ultimate Customer Experience," where he says we empower the consumer by educating them on the amazing benefits and incredible value. Show them what is in it for them. That is the motivating factor in saying "Yes." Jamie Cuthbert nails it!

"Let me buy vs. being sold

Communicate clearly (concise and precise)

Educate me---do not push me

Respect me---do not talk down to me (right tone)

Let me choose to work with you."

This is the right approach; rattling the price off and opting for hard selling is painful, as you sell to those customers for the last time.

Step up Your Customer Service Game by learning how to Overcome Objections

The payoff for improving your service processes is greater customer retention. Executing certain actions will prevent existing clients from leaving and grow others into loyal customers. To do this, every business interaction must be modeled on what has worked in the past and what is most likely to work in the future. These must be tailored to each buyer and their unique customer journey. What is better than acquiring a new customer? It is retaining an existing one. The churn rate is very high in the industry and needs to be stopped.

One of the most effective ways to do this is to overcome objections. This means determining what issues are preventing the client from saying "yes," addressing those objections and closing again.

If the client says:

"I just want an oil change; I will do the other things the next time."

Your response should be:

"Fixing the badly worn belt today could save you money in the event it breaks. Your vehicle can overheat, resulting in other costly repairs."

"It will not cost less to wait!"

"Doing it now could save you an additional trip."

"Replacing the leaking water pump will give you peace of mind."

"Not doing the transmission service, which is overdue based on the manufacturer's recommended interval, as well as the fluid condition, which is very dark and has a burnt odor, could void your warranty. From my experience, I recommend you protect your warranty."

"It takes just a few minutes to complete a credit card application, and in all likelihood, it'll be approved in the next fifteen minutes. Would you like to take advantage of this today?"

"The owner's manual indicates damage or failure due to neglect or lack of proper maintenance is not covered under the manufacturer's warranty."

Lowering the walls of consumers' objections is a critical part of being able to reach out and work with them for mutual success.

Listening is one of the most important skills. Countless advisors have to re-ask customers for their names. That is an embarrassment. Avoiding this requires a real focus on the client. This also means asking for clarification of spelling and/or having the advisor repeat the customer's requests and concerns to make sure they are in step with their issues. Meeting their expectations builds trust and integrity.

Do not cheat yourself. You can achieve stardom if you are committed to working on it — anyone who wants to succeed can. Remember, you are the only person who can stop you.

The Business Model for Preventative Maintenance

The secret is the constant investment into the training of your cast members, as value is what motivates the consumer. Secondly, the consumer needs a clear, concise, and precise understanding of the messages, the benefits that the service provides, and the value that the consumer gains by doing preventative maintenance. The greatest failure is service advisors stumbling with the message; they cut it short and blurt out the price. Hence, without value, the customer cannot see the reason for moving forward. If you know the word tracks, which are like training wheels, it helps prevent crashing. In the greatest percentage of cases, when you have flawless execution, the normal response will be, “Yes. How long will it take to complete this/these service(s)?”

Investing in the future by developing soft skills will greatly benefit the team. Offering and recommending preventative maintenance is the single best strategy for assisting the consumer in eliminating costly repairs. Looking back, having no issues with their vehicle will certainly enhance the strong desire to purchase that brand/model that has served them well.

If you are knowledgeable, you are in the same league as doctors helping people. We are in the business of helping people. It is not about selling them; our role is to empower the consumer by educating them with the ‘WIIFM’ so they understand and willingly open their wallets and share them with us.

Educating the consumer is the primary message that transfers value into the decision-making process, which becomes the motivating factor for consumers. Once the consumer clearly understands the amazing benefits and incredible value, it becomes equity. That is the deciding factor that consumers want. This is the winning formula for $ success; it is empowerment!

Financial Business Model, What a Great Opportunity!

The industry data suggest and support that maintenance should represent at least 50 % of your service business; some industry analysts suggest the bar should be higher, basically confirming a plus of the represented value.

Using a sample size of 15,000 annual visits to your location and using another piece of important data shows that consumers require 2.6 visits per year, which indicates that 5,769 are potential customers. (The wheel alignments are not included here since I have already provided breakout information on them in the chapter dealing with that subject). In one of these return visits, second maintenance is a possible consideration.

Let us examine the formula:

15,000 annual customers divided by 2.6 = 5,769 visits X $150 average price of mixed maintenance, (conservative)

5,769 X $150.00 = $865,350.00, with a margin of 30 points = $259,605 profit.

In many cases, it would be done by an apprentice. Thus, a lower labor cost.

$259,606.00 multiplied over 10 years could generate a projected profit of $2,596,060

Each of these financial business models indicates the importance of following the manufacturer's and aftermarket industry's best practice guidelines.

The Takeaway

I want to drill down to address the huge potential and the ultra-importance of doing maintenance:

1. The customer realizes that following the maintenance service interval schedule will extend the requirement for the service of a vehicle. However, keep in mind some systems still fail without any apparent reason.

2. Resale value is enhanced when you have a solid history of following the manufacturer's recommended service schedule. It provides a much higher comfort level for a potential buyer and, in many instances, is the single best-selling feature.

3. Completing the recommended service saves the owner a lot of money. An example is, that transmission with five or more shift points can become very expensive, i.e., $4K and up, which is not unusual.

4. Doing the maintenance as per schedule is a tenth of the cost (with some exceptions) when it comes to the automatic transmission.

5. The term WIIFM stands for "What is In It for me!" with 'me' being the consumer.

Since it is strongly supported by the manufacturer, failing to print out the maintenance service interval schedule gives it the hearsay status, and gives rise to failing to explain the findings to the customer. Two huge mistakes. come from the failure to print out the manufacturer's service interval schedule and the failure to explain before handing it over to the consumer.

The most significant secret to success is helping the consumer follow the manufacturer's preventative maintenance service interval schedule, regardless of which service is recommended. From my personal vehicle ownership experience, adhering to strict preventative maintenance has provided me with zero repair issues, whether related to radiators, heater cores, transmissions, transfer cases, differentials, power steering pumps, or hoses. Maintenance is a tenth of the cost of expensive repairs or even 5% in the case of major transmission work. Transmission specialty shops overpopulate the cities because the service industry, as a whole, has neglected to educate and empower consumers about the consequences of ignoring the service interval schedules. This is particularly true if their warranties expire.

Too often, the advisors short-cut the process; they fail to print out the manufacturer's interval service schedule; thus, they have nothing to show to the consumer to re-force the importance of getting the service done; they fail to have the necessary discussions with customers and are inefficient. Advisors need to share the amazing benefits and incredible value that these services provide. Your body language and your tone of voice need to be believable. Lastly, this statement needs to flow and roll off of one's tongue effortlessly. You cannot fake or stumble over the words. The biggest sin is the manager's lack of enforcing accountability.

When the steps of closing or asking are consistently well-executed by your staff, they should be able to score a closing rate of 80%. Your presentation must be professional and relevant while building a deeper relationship to gain additional trust. Leadership has to be very proactive by equipping and further investing in the careers of its cast members. You must challenge them, and motivate them with soft skills that are known as smart and power skills. To separate yourself from the best of the best, you need to up the game to win the day and the consumer.

CHAPTER 10

SECRETS TO OVERCOME OBJECTIONS AND WIN

"Every sale has five basic obstacles: no need, no money, no hurry, no desire, no trust."

– Zig Ziglar

Do You Hear "No" Too Many Times?

When it comes to selling, I like using the term educating because the consumers are motivated by value (WIIFM), which is the number one driver of a fantastic customer service experience and, therefore, sales. Right behind, at number two, is overcoming objections.

Consumers are crying out for more information. They are saying, "I require additional facts and information." Creating value by educating and empowering consumers with amazing benefits and substantial value will move consumers to say "Yes." The most significant reason for clients to say "No" is short-cutting the process, where the only information provided is typically the tech's note that is identified on the estimate. Many techs will leave one-line diagnostic comments, such as *"A ball joint is loose," "The tie rod is dangerously loose,"* or *"The power steering pressure line is leaking badly, and your power steering fluid is not visible on the dipstick."* Consumers need to be provided with clear, meaningful, and empowering statements delivered with confidence and conviction. Service advisors must use appropriate terminologies, such as "required," "recommended," and "preventative maintenance," as documented in the manufacturer's interval schedule. This schedule needs to be printed off and provided to the consumer. Many front-line advisors underestimate the power of the manufacturer's gospel.

Today, it is commonplace for consumers to respond with "No," and you can be certain your front line will hear it frequently. Objections, however, should be music to your ears. They are an open invitation to draw out concerns and discuss more information. In other words, ask the consumers what the real questions are. Let them know there are solutions to their problems. Slow down the conversation and use appropriate technical communication skills to overcome objections. Speak with calm authority and confidence without interrupting the customer because talking at the wrong time can backfire if you make an ill-timed attempt to win them over. The customer's first "No" may sound somewhat ridiculous, but if the advisors have abbreviated the process whereby little or no value has been communicated, it will surely shorten the interaction. Objections are a normal part of any sale, and if you are listening to the customer, they will be sending you a signal as to why; if they are not, it is your responsibility to find out. This is the opportunity to address the real issues that keep your clients from taking the recommended service or products. What they are communicating, in most cases, is, that you have not created enough benefits and value to motivate me to say "Yes." Value is created by sharing amazing benefits, outstanding features, and substantial value.

Consult the chapter on preventative maintenance. Memorizing the benefits will allow you to help the customer make the right decision. Educating the consumer by sharing the amazing benefits and the incredible added value is critical because consumers are motivated by value. When you hear an objection, you should realize the customer is probably saying, *"You haven't convinced (i.e., educated) me,"* so the service advisor must put more meat on the bone by drawing out the reason for the lingering doubts. Offer it again, educate, and ask for the business. Your attempt should be a flexible approach, and show empathy to close the sale. However, service advisors should know better than to never use pressure tactics to obtain the sale. Do not attempt to manipulate the customer to pursue a bargain or any other tactic that will burn the bridge for any future business. An objection is a legitimate request for more information. Sometimes, it may even come across a little comically or sarcastically, such as, *"You have got to be kidding me!"* or *"I wouldn't spend that kind of money!"* However, service advisors should be trained to deal with any such responses and should know what to say to help the customer.

I was once working with a team and overheard part of an attempted sales conversation, where I realized the consumer's response was a fearful "No." So, I asked the advisor what the consumer's concern was. He indicated that she did not want the service. The customer was in the waiting area, so I walked over to introduce myself and started a dialogue. I shared that I had witnessed the extremely dark condition of their vehicle's fluid and checked the service history. I printed out the manufacturer's interval schedule and then shared it with her, explaining the benefits and value of doing the service as well as the consequences of letting it pass. Somewhat to my surprise, she indicated that the advisor had not shared this information. He lacked confidence because he did not know the real benefits and values. Wow, what a teaching moment! Once I had shared the information, she gladly agreed to have the service completed and thanked me as well, because I provided the educational facts. She gave us her business because I had educated her and built trust, not by pressuring her but by being upfront and transparent about what needed to be done. The consumer comes to you wanting and needing help, and you should do just that.

By knowing how to overcome various objections, you will improve your close ratio by 25% or more and provide an example of what everyone is capable of doing. The fact of offering preventative maintenance service will also help close a sale.

Many people fail or lack information and vision. Today, we constantly need to invest in the cast members and teach them to offer a good and helpful solution to the consumers. Many rank-and-file service managers do not understand the manufacturers' reasoning for preventative maintenance. As some techs believe, it is a money grab; it is unbelievable that they are still in the industry. The wrong or abbreviated process creates confusion and chaos. This is why word tracks are so essential because they will guide you in effectively communicating the benefits and values consumers need to understand. They come to you in need of help, so you must be sincere and refrain from taking advantage of their circumstances. If the consumer is saying "No" and you do nothing, you do a disservice to them by merely accepting their "No" when you have indicated that the repair is required due to a safety issue, or because Recommended Preventative Maintenance is needed.

If left unaddressed, an expensive repair is just around the corner. If your staff are not prepared to commit to the process, primarily due to lack of training, the consumer will lose confidence and seek out your competition, which may be better equipped to provide more information, the benefits and value, and a positive, reassuring approach that will win them over.

Let me discuss an example. A customer calls because he/she thinks they have "heard a noise" and is enquiring about the cost of diagnosing it (which should include a road test). Offer this client a free, no-charge road test and full mechanical inspection. To win big, invest in an amazing AutoServe1, as it builds trust and provides a stunning inspection with photographic evidence supporting the service recommendation. This will be in a real-time setting, that can be immediately sent to their cell phone. It is powerful and impactful, which is an excellent opportunity to gain their confidence and obtain additional repairs or services. The secret is to create a high level of value and a quality repair service. If the consumer has drivability concerns, a reasonably lengthy road test is required to confirm that all the concerns and issues have been completely addressed.

A seasoned service manager must hold all staff accountable in the pursuit of excellence. Their goal should be to take every possible step to provide over-the-top quality, thus exceeding the consumer's expectations. They must take the necessary time to place that vehicle in the winner's circle. This process is always critical. Despite objections, the customer's vehicle repairs will have to be completed at some point or other. If you fail to address their grievances, then some other auto service providers will be rewarded with that work.

One reason service advisors are afraid to respond to objections is the natural fear of rejection. The fear issue can cause advisors to drop the conversation. It helps to observe them as they often lack confidence. Objections are uncomfortable simply because supervisors have failed to equip their staff with valuable insight that addresses all of these delay tactics. Service advisors have to up their game and commit to learning the materials that address the various concerns as they are powerful in winning over the consumer. Call service advisors into your office and address the problems and provide them with the necessary insight as homework, such as reading these chapters over many times.

Expand the memory muscles with what are initially considered hard words. It takes practice to polish your approach until it flows out of your mouth. Have the right body language, the right tone of voice, and that inner confidence, and have the killer instinct to convert prospects into potential customers. Know that your insight is part of who you are, help the customers out without the high pressure or other tactics, and deliver the message without that ugly attitude.

When you ask these advisors why their efforts are lacking, you will find it comes back to not knowing the power of knowledge. They do not understand or have not attempted to build those required skills in their memory banks. Again, this is due to service managers lacking accountability for their teammates. Solving this means having proactive service managers (or consultants) who will teach essential word tracks that help their people become more confident. It is like asking for that first date: the question is sometimes awkward and requires the right insightful approach to bring value, which will add to your confidence. Advisors need to embrace hearing "No"; it is seldom personal. Fear is often an artificial concern. To help staff, a proactive service manager must be coaching and mentoring the cast members. Coaching is challenging when the service manager is continuously in his or her office and not spending time on the front line. Immediately after the consumer departs, while the conversation is fresh in mind, ask the staffer to sit down and debrief them, laying out the exact process to address any weaknesses. It should be the advisor's goal to become more knowledgeable and to be next in line for a promotion to becoming a supervisor or an assistant service manager.

Occasionally, consumers turn to objections to avoid making a decision. Interject by asking if they need a moment to call someone in the family to get an opinion, or better yet, do a Digital Vehicle Inspection, which will provide the pictures/videos that offer insight and information helping to bring this to the top of mind. If it is a college student, they may have financial concerns or need advice. Be sure to deal with such customers politely and educate them about all the possible options they can opt for when it comes to payment or suggest they ask someone they trust, like family or a friend, to advise them on the issue. Under normal circumstances, practically every repair or service will get worse if ignored. It will not magically cure itself, and there is a good chance it will become more expensive sooner than later. If the customer is already thinking about it but is hesitant to proceed, this indicates that the service advisor has not addressed the actual benefit and value of the necessary work. Assuring consumers that you have been in business for some time and providing legitimate (reliable) service ensures their return and becoming part of your valued clientele.

Customers understand they will have to have the work done somewhere by someone, but advisors often take the easy way out and drop the sales process. The rewards can be great, but most staffers and service managers back away from this part of the job because they do not want to come across as pushy or do not have the experience and insight to walk the customer through the process. This is where common sense is needed. Consider it another learning experience that life has to offer.

"You have seen the severe need for the repairs, but You will have one of the best techs working on it. We offer great warranty and the highest quality parts, competitively, since we do an annual competitive shopping of our competitors within our community."

"Based on this information, we have confirmed that we have all the parts and can complete this repair by day's end. Will this work for you?"

Objections allow you to become partners in the maintenance of your customers' vehicles. You have to build this relationship with integrity and straightforward communication, which will lead to loyal customers for years to come. Clients will quickly realize if you are interested in finding a solution for them and allowing their problems to become your problems.

The conversations with clients must be held with the utmost respect, with the client's best interests at heart. It should not come across as a hard sell or an exaggeration of a small problem into a major safety concern. There is such a great opportunity to resolve existing customer concerns by finding a solution to the issue at hand.

Objections are merely buying signals: *"I am interested in what you are saying; however, I do not have enough information, or I do not clearly understand enough to authorize you to proceed."* You may have to ask questions that allow the client to express their concerns or uncover missed points they are unclear about. Hang in there. Continue the dialogue, so they get on the same page. If you do not the service advisor will end up being viewed as the bearer of bad news, which experience indicates, is just a matter of time. Advisors may give half-hearted presentations or have wishy-washy attitudes and may lack real understanding and substance. Their body language may communicate very little confidence. This is why the tone of voice and how one delivers the message are key. Clients will read into it that you are not sold or confident. So, work on demonstrating your confidence. Learn to share in a manner that you are educating the consumer. Spend time working at it and rehearsing with yourself or seek out help from the service manager.

Gartner's research has shown:

When it comes to making a purchase, 64% of people find customer experience more important than price.

Objections Fall into Four Categories

- Price, Risk, Budget, or ROI
- Quality of the repairs, service, or product
- Relationship and or Trust
- Time or stalling

What Are the Key Points to Addressing These Objections?

- Agree with the consumer.
- Address the issues.

- Educate the consumer so they clearly understand "what is in it for me." Value is what motivates people. Share the amazing benefits and incredible value.
- Advance them through the closing stages.

1. Price, Risk, Budget, ROI

If the advisor has fully explained the benefits, features, and value to the consumers, they will be willing to open their wallets because this is what motivates them. Consumers will push back if they are daunted by the price. It requires the service advisor to break down the cost based on the actual value, which will entail laying out a much larger sum of money when visiting another dealer later. They must realize, at that point, that they will have to consider much more seriously their cash flow and where the money will come from. Again, offer third-party financial assistance with a previously arranged QR scan that will extend credit in 10 minutes or so. Often, this is a game-changer.

Like many companies, the solution is to offer a short or longer-term interest-free (or no-payment) period of time and provide the customer with a short, quick application process. This often resolves the issue of timing, which differs for most people. Surprise repairs often leave them feeling vulnerable. In such a situation, do not judge your customer; ask questions that help address their issues. It is important to empathize and assure them that you will do whatever is possible to build trust, loyalty, and goodwill. Quality matters, much more than a lower price. That is where value wins the day. Shop your competitors, pull the data together, know where you stand, and share it with the consumer. Many times, your rivals' equipment, processes, products, and services will not match up to yours. On such occasions, You will know you have created value.

Script for Price Objections

"I agree the price is more than you had in mind to spend, but based on experience, cheap work costs more in the end, unlike quality service that lasts. I think both of us recognize that value is what you want. My tech can have this done within the next 50 minutes. Does this work for you?"

2. Quality of Repairs, Service, and Product

Quality is a core issue, particularly in circumstances where consumers are already stressed to the limit. With today's availability of information, customers will want to do their investigation about different shops' workmanship and what is involved in a specific repair or service. Once they understand that repeated repairs down the road will be more expensive than quality work done right the first time, cost becomes less of an issue, and their problems can be resolved. However, product and service quality cannot and should not remain a concern in their mind at the end of your interaction with them. They have to know they will be receiving the best.

Script for Quality of the Repair

"I agree that the quality of the service and parts is important. You do not want to experience this again in a short period. We both acknowledge quality serves your best interests now and in the future. I have checked our inventory, and I can have this repair completed

before closing the shop. Does this work for you to have the repair completed right away?"

3. Relationship and Trust

This is an incredibly important aspect of your organization, and it depends on investing in the training of front-line advisors. The questions consumers will ask about your legitimacy or credibility will hinge on what is shared by your staff.

Consumers will frequently be overwhelmed when having to make decisions based solely on price without knowing the real value or WIIFM. They will zone out while thinking about whether they can afford everything the advisor is rattling off or if They will have to commute without the vehicle they rely on.

The attitude of your staff sometimes comes off the wrong way. The key is to avoid appearing defensive and, instead, empathize with the consumer.

When your priority is to exceed customer service expectations, it rids you of all the trappings that bog down the business. The major difference between the top 20/80 groupings is the visionary leadership skill sets of service managers who can respond instantaneously to difficult situations. An investment in the right people with the right skill sets is as important as advanced AI equipment and other smart devices.

Script for Relationship and Trust Objections

"I agree the reason you are back is that we have a very good relationship. By coming to someone you know very well shows the trust that we have served you well. You know the quality of our service in the past, and our very competitive price has provided you with a positive experience. Since we have had a good relationship, I trust we can move forward since I always have your best interests in mind. Does this work for you since the tech can complete it ASAP? Should I inform him to get you going within the next hour?"

4. Time and Stalling

Consumers stall for many reasons, such as money issues, not having time, being unconvinced that the service is necessary, or needing more time to shop around and answer questions. Thus, it is the service advisors' responsibility to know all the right things to say when addressing these issues. While educating them, advisors need to display confidence and not be defensive in the process.

In some cases, a spouse may need to check with their husband or wife about the household budget (which frequently means the wife, since, in a large percentage of married couples, That is who manages the money). If That is the case, it makes sense to explain the different plans that can bridge their financial issues. Simply asking questions will show the path forward. We sell time to diagnose problems similar to a doctor who takes time to transition from one question to the next before making a diagnosis.

Script for Time and Stalling Objections

"I agree, time is money, and I'm concerned that if you do not address this engine coolant leak, there is a chance you could overheat the engine and incur much greater costs and inconvenience. We both agree you have already lost income due to the delays you have experienced. Would you agree you have wasted enough time and money, and now it is become a much greater issue? Does it make sense that doing these repairs now is in your best interest?"

"Do you have any other concerns that need attention?"

"I noticed your oil change sticker is due. Would you like to take advantage of doing it now?"

"If there are any other concerns to be addressed, our certified technician will complete a peace of mind digital inspection at no charge."

After the primary concern has been addressed and a DVI (digital vehicle inspection) has been completed, text it to the consumer; this is a vital step/progress. Then, move on to other required additional repairs and Preventative Maintenance, since 80% of vehicles require them.

If you have commented on how well the vehicle has been maintained (by listing some of those items), you can then say:

"However, the tech wanted me to share a couple of concerns that require your attention."

(For example)

"Your brake hoses are badly cracked and require replacement for safety reasons."

"The brake fluid failed the industry test, showing too much copper/moisture, so the tech is recommending a brake fluid flush that brings it back to the manufacturer's specs."

"The cost of the front brake hoses is XX dollars for parts and labor, and the brake fluid exchange and flushing of contaminated fluids cost XX dollars in the package price."

Using an industry-approved test strip is a great show and tell.

Overcoming Objections Financial Business Model

Let us assume that your annual traffic is 10,000 visits. Let us say that 50% of the consumers raise objections. And the No. 1 cause for consumers declining a service, (i.e., price in itself) brings little or no value.

Here is the math based on history:

5,000 consumers with a 50% buy-in:

$150.00 (door-rate) x 2500 per R.O. = $375,000 X 10 years = $3,750,000

10,000 consumers with a 50% buy-in:

$150.00 (door-rate) X 5000 per R.O. = $750,000 X 10 years = $7,500,000

The impact of $375,000 X 30% margin = $112,500 in profit X 10 years = $1,125,000

The impact of $750,000 X 30% margin = $225,000 in profit X 10 years = $2,250,000

The Takeaway

Regardless of the sale objections, you can overcome them with the confidence displayed by your body language and specific words communicated clearly to the customers. Be real and deliver your presentation without rushing the process. Be deliberate in creating credible value and amazing benefits that they can take to the bank.

The core secret is to ask the right questions. Discover what is behind customer objections, so you provide the right solutions to the issues that confront them.

The payoff comes when you invest in your cast members and train them on how to overcome objections. Sometimes, the consumer provides little or no information, so the service advisor has to ask them outright, so They will know what is holding them back. Now use the material in this chapter to interact with the consumer and make it happen. Fear sets in when you have failed in rehearsing; put in the time and reward yourself, and You will see your fears melt away. Be encouraged to put in the work, be confident that You will nail it, and you will become a superstar. The secret is knowing the word tracks so you can effectively respond to turn an objection into a score. The other secret is educating the consumer on the amazing benefits and incredible value; when consumers clearly understand 'what is in it for me,' they will be motivated to proceed. One last thing to keep in mind is to be concise and precise about the consequences of <u>not</u> proceeding with the service.

How to Deliver a Million-dollar Opportunity

You, as a service advisor, are the face and the voice of your incredible brand; it is the right time to up your game by delivering an exceptional customer experience that outperforms all those within the marketplace. It comes back to investing in training while improving the already high standard of excellence by investing in the cast members. It is about recharging their batteries, bringing new energy and more emotional connection into the relationship.

Your presentation must be personal, professional, and relevant while building a deeper relationship to gain the additional trust of the consumer. Leadership has to be very proactive by equipping and further investing in their career of excellence. You must challenge them, and motivate them with soft skills that are known as smart and power skills. To separate yourself from the best of the best, you need to up your game to win the day and the consumer.

Acknowledgement: *Material used in chapter 11, obtained from the article titled 'RESPECT' published on Ask.Patty.com. was used with permission. I would also like to acknowledge Jody DeVere, CEO of AskPatty.com Inc., for her co-operation in this regard. A permission letter stating their consent has been attached and can be found in the appendix section of the book.*

NOTES

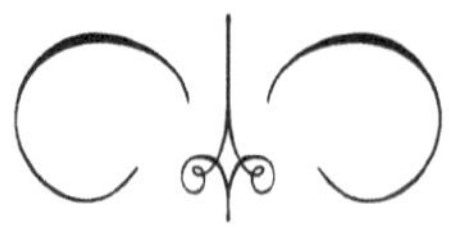

Chapter 11
R-E-S-P-E-C-T

"Empower people to lead with purpose, vision, and influence to enable greatness in themselves and others."

-Unknown

How can you make your shop more attractive to women consumers and attract and retain female employees? Simple. By showing R-E-S-P-E-C-T.

For many shops, hiring women is about putting forward an atmosphere of friendliness and trustworthiness, particularly to women customers, who, as we all know, account for 85% of all purchase decisions.

It turns out that hiring women involves more than just appearances. Studies such as "The Case for Investing in Women" (tinyurl.com/hirewomen), a report released in 2014 by the Anita Borg Institute (ABI), contains some impressive research on women in business. Other studies by organizations such as McKinsey & Company, Catalyst, and Columbia University have shown that companies that attract and hire women employees are quantifiably more successful than companies that do not. However, what I hear most often from shop owners and hiring managers is that women do not apply for jobs as technicians, customer service staff, or service advisor positions. Anecdotal comments I hear from women and shop owners are that they often do not get hired as technicians because they "will not fit in with the guys in the back" or because shops fear sexual harassment and other legal issues associated with hiring women. In 2017, women held just 25% of all the positions in the automotive industry, including manufacturing. With this in mind, it will take a concerted and sustained effort to attract, hire, and retain women - but it is worth the effort. Check out this list of 10 ways provided by AskPatty.com and Jody DeVere to make your business more attractive to women (consumers and potential employees) to make it more successful.

1. Create a Female-friendly Culture

Previous poor treatment and lack of respect for female job candidates - and women customers, for that matter - leaves a negative, lasting impression on how women perceive the industry. It is difficult to believe that in some repair shops, women are still greeted with a detestable statement such as, *"Is your husband with you today?"* Thus, service providers are advised to commit to providing a consistent, female-friendly culture and experience.

2. Provide New and Ongoing Training

Statistics show that there is an increase in the number of women interested in pursuing automotive careers. To attract these women, work with your local automotive trade schools, as well as your high school career fairs and apprenticeship programs. In addition to that, provide scholarships for women and offer to include ongoing training and education with financial support in your compensation plans. This will give you a competitive advantage in hiring and retraining women and, in fact, all of your new employees.

3. Create a Career Path

Re-examine the positions in your company that effectively interest and challenge women and encourage their entry into the industry, as well as in making it their career.

4. Offer Flexible Schedules

Consider not just the primary financial needs of full and part-time women employees but also their families and personal needs. Millennial men and women who have children want a career that offers a flexible work schedule that allows them to participate in their children's school events and after-school activities.

5. Commit to Mentoring

Make it a point to formally mentor women employees. And, as an owner, you need to invest in their careers by allowing them to attend conferences such as the 'Women in Auto Care' biannual events. A national organization comprised of auto care professionals dedicated to providing opportunities, education, and career leadership to women in the industry, 'Women in Auto Care,' offers a formal mentoring program, as well as opportunities to learn and network with other women who want to build their careers in the automotive industry.

6. Make Them Part of the Team

Shake off the old "We have always done it this way" approach and try new methods. Explore realistic ways to meet the needs of female employees. Challenge and eliminate the thinking and procedures that have been used forever and adapt to the changing trends in the industry.

7. Actively Listen to Their Thoughts.

You must understand that the female perspective is essential to your business. Ask for their opinions and listen when you are conducting your job interview with them. After you have hired a woman, keep an open mind. You might be surprised at the great insight about marketing, selling, serving, and communicating better with women customers that she will bring to your team. (*DF - The data certainly supports that claim, and we should be buying in. In my experience, they control the financial purse strings and much more.*)

8. Support Women in Your Local Market

You can send a strong message to the women in your community by supporting groups such as the Girl Scouts, the National Association of Women Business Owners (NAWBO), and other local charities that support women's issues or health concerns. Networking with your local women's organizations creates a pool of potential employees from which to hire. (*DF - this involvement, or through a small ad of support that supports women's events and activities, would be a positive step in bringing additional traffic to one's business).*

9. Include This in Help-wanted Ads

When placing advertisements for potential new hires, carefully craft job descriptions to include job experiences that match fields where women traditionally have had work experience. Doing so sends a strong signal to women job seekers that you will welcome them in your shop. And, of course, place these ads in the customer service or retail categories where women with the right experience will see them, as well as in the "automotive category" of online job services such as Indeed, Monster, etc. (*DF – as well as LinkedIn, etc.)*

10. Highlight Women in Your Business

Prominently feature your women employees – their photos, profiles, roles, and responsibilities - on your social media network. Again, You will be telling a great story to women consumers and potential employees that you value women's skills, abilities, and buying power. Women spend thrice more time on social media, per day than men. Facebook ads aimed especially at women that tell this story serve as an effective tool to advertise and promote open positions to women job seekers. Make a long-term commitment to attract, hire, and retain more women. You will realize higher profits, gain a strategic marketing advantage, and increase your retention rate with women customers.

THE TAKEAWAY

I realized, by doing an internal audit of analysis of the gender demographics, that the 20-plus years-of-age female gender lead by 51-49%. In addition, they have always spent a good portion of the day being directly involved with the consumers. I have witnessed that in many cases the wife/partner was the one who controlled and authorized the need for repairs. This confirms that the female gender is the 'power broker' in the family unit.

Time Magazine's 2018 edition cover titled: 'The Richer Sex' by author Lisa Mundy, predicted that women's economic rise was above that of men, called the "The Big Flip"; it is one of several cutesy terms she uses, along with "breadwomen" (her words for female "breadwinner") which will benefit everyone.

"Women's earnings will not only bring about a new liberation for women but also for men," she writes, "More women will marry down; more men will marry up."

Women hold 51% of the jobs in "management, professional and related occupations," according to the Bureau of Labor Statistics. Education is a woman's game; women earn 57% of bachelor's degrees and makeup 60% of graduate students.

I believe we need to get out of our comfort zone. Only then will we be able to see more, become more, achieve more, and win more. I desire to challenge you as well as encourage you to get out of that comfort zone so you can be more successful; you need to put some extra pressure on yourself to become an extraordinary individual who has that burning desire for excellence, to become a high achiever and get out of that bubble. Only then can you become the superstar of your liking. I trust this book will inspire you and motivate you to put in that extra effort to become the best possible version of yourself.

NOTES

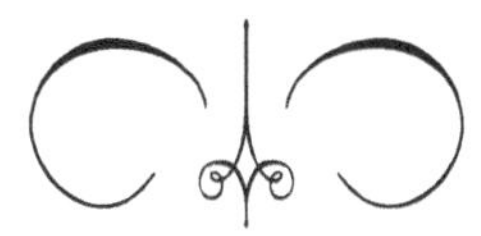

Chapter 12

Character Traits of Effective Leaders

"If you focus on results, you will never change; if you focus on change, you will get results."

-Jack Dixon

"Courage does not always roar. Sometimes, it is the quiet voice at the end of the day saying, 'I will try again tomorrow.'"

-Mary Anne Radmacher

Leaders Must Become Influencers by Investing in Cast Members

True leaders positively influence others around them and uphold a professional demeanor in all situations. I watch leaders whom I respect and observe how they lead and ask them for advice when faced with a challenge. Leadership is about making decisions and being confident in those decisions. Our greatest achievement is in investing in our cast members so, by strength, the organization can be divided into a lot of different areas. The most critical area is the front line; these people are the voice and the face of the organization. This is the most challenging position within any automotive setting. Yet, when the cast members are fully equipped, they totally understand and inform or educate the consumers accordingly; thus, generating an amazing customer service experience. The consistent and predictable services create a memorable experience. When the cast members have been empowered objectively, it leaves the customers feeling 'Wow!' as the service was above and beyond their expectations.

History indicates that a percentage of auto service departments do exceptionally well. Some auto service departments have generated up to 47% of the balance sheet by the labor sales and back parts being installed. Considering this high margin, departments can certainly impact the overall P&L picture. Many auto services have a functional role in attempting to care for consumers purchasing a vehicle. There is a percentage of auto service centers that do not generate profits and need to be subsidized by other departments.

Doing a Competitive Market Analysis

During my time in the automotive service industry, every single year, I would shop at the competition's store in my trading area, with a blocked number, to inquire what the actual door charge-out rate was. Secondly, I would check prices for maintenance service items since, in many cases, it is a combined parts and labor number for each maintenance service (smooth pricing or menu price). In my city,

I would check in with OEM dealers who meet in February on an annual basis as a group to discuss the raising of the door rate as well as a few other agendas. I could predict the timing of that event and make the calls for the updates.

The purpose of this was clearly to understand what was happening within my trading area. The secondary purpose was to have that fingertip knowledge about what is transpiring in one's market area because my desire was not to leave any money on the table. I always wanted to be competitive and have a very strong balance sheet. That is why we invest in a business, regardless of whether it is OEM, chains or franchises, or independents. I was just surprised by the number of times the business had a not-so-great balance sheet. I was shocked; my greatest pride and joy was to produce an above-average balance sheet based on solid margins. All of these are fixable and doable situations. During my many years as a consultant, I found that a large percentage of the chain and independent service outlets failed to investigate what was transpiring in their immediate market area. In most of the stores where I was consulting, when the door rate was changed, the staff was not even aware that the hourly door rate had changed or that some of the menu prices had been adjusted. Only one part-time staff realized the wheel alignment price had increased and brought it to my attention; the rest had not noticed, which was surprising. Nor did even one consumer notice the change.

When you bump up your charge-out rate, this immediately impacts the balance sheet. The biggest expense line on the balance sheet is the cost of labor. It is critically important that the cost is controlled to reflect a solid balance sheet in the high 20 and into the 30 points plus. In Fort McMurray, there were only four OEM dealers, along with one independent and chain store. I called around these four stores and very quickly realized that their charge-out rate was $300.00 an hour. During my price shopping, I asked, *"How soon could I book my vehicle for some service?"* The response was 4 weeks, which left me shocked!

The chain store was charging $150.00 an hour; with not too deep a dive, I realized how two of the problems could be immediately solved and addressed. One concern was they could not retain technicians, which was not very productive since they were leaving for a much more attractive offer. What I did was a bold move. We immediately upped the door rate by $75.00. In the eyes of the consumer, this was not even on their radar. The consumers just wanted timely vehicle service, and the price was not an issue for them.

So, the management team met with the technicians to inform them that their hourly pay was going to be increased by $20.00. Before the end of the week, I recommended another $50.00 increase to the charge-out hourly rate, which bumped up the actual hourly rate as well. So, the new actual hourly charge-out jumped to $325.00, and the technician's hourly pay increased by $35.00. So, with this increase, the store was attracting more technicians and no more labor shortage issues.

The store had 13 service bays, and now we had technicians in every bay along with part-time technicians to fill evenings and Saturdays. So, this fixed the balance sheet, and with this small exercise, this store had the single largest percentage of increase over the next full year. The other reward was, with $125.00 for each billable hour, this store rocketed to the top of the chain. Here are the two big wins; the $125.00 increase is the retail charge-out rate average for the greatest percentage of the stores within the chain of nearly 500 stores. The $35.00 increase at that time also worked out to be the mean average as well. It is like the old saying, 'location, location, location.' Then, by applying the principles discussed in each chapter, the store was also fine-tuned to further double-digit impact growth, and by managing each area, the impact was compounding, and the bottom line on the balance sheet was dramatically impacted.

Implementing these proven strategies and best practices has an immediate and powerful impact on the balance sheet and allows the CEO to invest in the right artificial intelligence tool for even greater growth. All too often, I hear that AI and smart tools are considered a cost rather than a resounding bottom line impacter that continues year after year, and the growth in sales and profits is evident.

I have done it, and I have witnessed others doing likewise. The return on investment (ROI) is a gigantic turnaround. It is a win for the consumer because they love AI and smart tools as it eliminates the past old-school approaches of hard-selling and helps consumers feel empowered and comfortable through an educational approach. Often, these mentioned tools dramatically change the consumer mindset from not so sure to seeing the importance without persuasion and zero manipulation. These tools are game changers whereby consumers sell themselves.

The service business has to mirror the retail, which is, 'let me buy' versus 'being sold to' (changing the mindset in the service center from selling to buying). Once again, there needs to be a mindset shift similar to that of the retail business: 'Let me buy,' or 'Let me choose.' Communicate concisely and precisely to be clear. Educate them well, so they sell themselves and see what is in it for them.

Respect Me - Never Talk Down to Me

Without question, leadership is the key to pulling everything together; visionary leaders see things that others may overlook. A visionary leader is a person who has a clear idea of how the future should look. They set out concrete steps to bring a vision to life, and then they lead a team of people in that direction.

Traits of an Effective Leader

On the Floor

This comes with having the confidence and knowledge to understand the key performance indicators that consistently generate growth in sales. It also means coaching to deliver a customer service experience that exceeds the consumer's expectations. You have to be quick on your feet and have your finger on the pulse of the business throughout the day.

To me, this means having heart-to-heart conversations with employees, asking them where they want to be in five or ten years. Then you must support them and lay out a plan. You will get more return from your investment in staff than you can imagine.

A visionary leader is a person who has a clear idea of how the future should look. They set out concrete steps to bring a vision to life, and then they lead a team of people in that direction.

Strategic

Strategic planning is a skill many visionary leaders possess. They can envision what they want the future to look like and then strategize on how to get there. Since they are not detail-oriented, the strategic plan may not include all the technicalities, but it will be a starting point for the big picture.

Risk-taking

Visionary leaders understand risks, and they are willing to take them.

Organized

They are highly organized and pay close attention to the team they gather around them. Often, visionary leaders are highly involved in systems analysis to determine who should be doing what, when, and how often.

Focused

Visionary leaders can maintain focus. Once the goal is identified, the leader starts taking steps to reach it, even when that means changing the minds of others around them. They work hard to display the characteristics they want to see in their team.

Magnetic

Visionaries draw people to them with a welcoming, open persona that brings out the best qualities in those around them.

Collaborative

Visionary leaders know that team members' buy-in is much more readily achieved when everyone is invited to participate in the creative process. They use the strengths of their team members to balance their weaknesses, and they embrace creativity and new ideas.

Innovative

Visionaries have a great imagination. They are not afraid to ask "what if," and they instill a love for that question in those around them.

Open-minded

Even if they are dedicated to the big picture in their minds, they can be flexible about reaching that vision. They can assimilate information from many sources to develop more creative solutions.

Emotionally Intelligent

Not only are visionary leaders intelligent in the traditional sense of the word, but they are also emotionally intelligent. They understand the power of feelings and are capable of showing empathy to those around them.

Confident

Leaders have to be confident individuals as their decisions directly affect their organization. A leader has to have the right amount of confidence and faith in his capabilities and skills to the point that no outside noise can smudge it. They are huge risk-takers, and they have to ensure their win every time to lead an organization toward success.

Competitive

Leaders are usually competitive by nature. And this personality trait, more often than not, serves as a motivation for them. Their striving to be the best in the market makes them push themselves to the limit and think outside the box, which ultimately leads them to a unique perspective.

Killer Instincts

Visionary leaders have killer instincts as they conduct a competitive market analysis, and before implementing any strategy, they approach it from all possible aspects, once they find answers to all their queries, they implement it within their organization and ensure that all the relevant staff and team members are made aware of it.

Inspirational

You can find visionaries quoted in motivational speeches and self-help books. They know how to make us passionate about a goal or vision.

Challenges of Being a Visionary Leader

Big-picture leaders may miss important details. Some visionaries can force themselves to develop the ability to focus on details, but this is rare. For this reason, it is much more common for visionary leaders to hire detail-oriented people to work closely with them.

Those with a visionary management style may sacrifice present-day circumstances for the idea of the future. They may ignore important issues that need their attention at the moment because they are so future-oriented.

Visionary leaders may miss other opportunities because they are focused on one goal. They may refuse to change the plan or abandon it, even when it does not make sense anymore.

Best Practices of Visionary Leaders

There are many good practices that visionary leaders exhibit, as per the examples discussed in the following paragraphs.

Value of Plan

Good visionary leaders understand the value of a mission statement. They know how it can solidify the vision among team members. They begin a project with a contemplated plan that includes everything, from processes to staff analysis.

Value Improvement

Visionary leaders are always looking for improvement. They actively seek out opportunities to create buy-ins from employees by improving company structures.

Know Their Timing

Visionary leaders share the vision with the right people at the right time. They invite others to give input and ideas so the vision is shared and the creative process is not just limited to one person.

Tips For Becoming a Visionary Leader

Whatever your natural tendencies, you can learn to adopt a more visionary leadership style. Here are a few visionary leadership traits to start practicing:

Keep Calm and Be Consistent

In any period of change, conflict is bound to come up. In times of conflict, practice deep breaths or step away if you need to. It is better to take time to process the issue than to react out of emotion.

Empathize

Empathy is an important part of leadership and vital to good communication. Try viewing things from a different perspective, even if you do not like the point of view.

Practice Good Communication Skills

Maintaining eye contact and asking clarifying questions are key when communicating with others. Pay attention to the physical cues of the person you are talking to. Look for signals that you are being understood and well-received, and be sure to keep your body language friendly and welcoming.

Be Assertive

If you are asking someone to buy into your vision for the future, you need to do so with confidence while still being respectful. Work on maintaining an even tone of voice and setting forth concrete assertions.

A Leader Must Be Competent

You may have a likable personality, but that does not mean you automatically have what it takes to run a shop – especially a medium-to-large operation. If the leader is figuring out what to do on the fly, most advisors and techs will sense weakness and take advantage. This is a game they will play, put you in a difficult spot, and the team will be fractured. There is a lot of turnover among service managers due to techs, and without proper training, they will revert to old habits, and the manager will be vulnerable.

People Development

Beyond technical skills, companies seek leaders who are "fast and flexible" and empowered to act proactively. The auto industry has a perceived shortage of commercially oriented executives with business development expertise who can simultaneously see all aspects of the business, the bigger industry, and the economic picture and operate within a complex organizational matrix. Being flexible and nimble has proven to be more important than being big to compete and win in this environment. To build a more intelligent organization, automotive firms are working to develop people who understand how to receive and circulate information with autonomy and initiative, i.e., an internal intelligent network.

Knowledgeable Service Manager

Service managers must be extremely knowledgeable, fully committed, completely invested, and engaged. They must be visionaries, masters of detail, great listeners, and outstanding mentors, able to resolve touchy, difficult situations with fairness. They should never lose sight of the front line or technical training in the back shop that ensures accountability to do things right the first time. To be successful, leaders must provide a positive, challenging message that is motivational clear, concise, and precise. To me, this means having heart-to-heart conversations with employees, asking them where they want to be in five or ten years. Then you must support them and lay out a plan. You will get more return from your investment in staff than you can imagine.

Leader Must Be Decisive and Clear

You do everyone a favor when you say what needs to be said instead of sugar-coating an issue. Being brutally honest can save you time, money, and energy. A leader must be consistent. You must treat everyone as you would wish to be treated. You must be clear about your high customer service expectations and desire for loyalty. You must be disciplined to avoid Jekyll-and-Hyde scenarios.

Prove yourself every day, not just when your back is against the wall and time is running out. Do things right at all times, not simply when the boss is watching, when you feel like it, or when it is easy, cheap, popular, or convenient.

Leaders Must Maintain Accountability

They must ensure high-quality diagnostics and functional, lengthy road tests. If a service manager allows this to become sporadic, problems will surface quickly.

A Leader Must Have a Strong Work Ethic

A leader must have the wisdom and energy for this responsibility. Having an ethical character is a must, as is a dedication to work that goes beyond regular hours and demands. Are you willing to go the extra daily mile, not just when a staff member calls in sick or is on vacation?

Mental Toughness

Mental toughness is a personality trait that determines your ability to perform consistently under stress and pressure and is closely related to character, resilience, grit, and perseverance.

Strong Leaders Are Forward-thinking

Leaders should have the vision to drive the customer service experience, which, more than anything, impacts sales growth and profits. These people are the cleanup hitters.

In "Are You a Leader Worth Following," Dave Anderson's June 25, 2014 post on dealerelite.net says:

"A title does not make you a leader; it simply buys you time to become one.

It is foolish to believe anyone has been made more competent by a change in title.

Leadership is performance, not position; it is a daily choice you make, not a special place at a conference table where you sit.

Do not assume you have followers; you may only have subordinates. How you act as a leader determines whether a subordinate converts to a follower; subordinates comply whereas a follower is more likely to commit."

While leaders must put others first in business, they must not place themselves above the owners. If you want to lead, you must earn your stripes. Hiring the proper individuals is crucial, so giving preference to close friends or family can disrupt the healthy team dynamics that are essential. When you have identified someone with next-generation leadership potential, it is wise to provide them with access to senior-level meetings. This allows leaders to pinpoint their suitability for a key management role when the position becomes available.

A good leader will recognize talent early, so they are ready when called upon.

Service Advisors Must Lead in Training

Service advisors have to note consumer concerns so they do not infect the business's culture. During training visits, I witnessed advisors being satisfied with (and techs acting on) vague customer information due to a lack of communication. Advisors need to restate consumers' specific concerns so their problems are understood. Furthermore, this helps in explaining the issues to their associates.

Leaders must have accountability

Leaders who maintain accountability make certain that team members use proper, powerful terms such as *required* and *recommended.* The impact of these words is greater than you can imagine. They will also insist on accountability to the customer. If a team member is contacting a customer via phone or text, they should confirm that it is the right person, and record their name, the time, the cost, and make notes on the repair order. This avoids any misunderstanding if someone else picks up the vehicle or calls in.

Leaders must be teachable. Leadership does not mean one is relegated to being a coach or mentor and ceases to be a learner; those who are not learning are not growing. Leaders must work on themselves. How many leadership books do you read each year? Do you attend outside effective training courses and conferences to keep yourself sharp and ahead of your competition?

Leaders have to be open to feedback to learn. Otherwise, they become afflicted with arrogance and condescending attitudes. People respect and love leaders who act like the teachers who empower them by investing in them.

Dave Anderson, about the qualities of accepting responsibility and developing human potential, says:

"Does the buck stop with you, or when things go awry, do you whip out your black belt in blame and point to other people or conditions to excuse your failures? Do you admit mistakes and share what you learned from them with your team? Little is more disheartening for a follower than to have a whiney, sniffling victim as a boss.

Do people grow under your leadership? Are you a consistent coach, trainer, and mentor? Do you provide the tools and opportunities people need to reach their potential? Would your people say that you are more likely to stretch them more than maintain them? How many of your people have been promoted in the past two, five, or ten years? Leaders are in the stretching business. If you are not consistently leaving people better than you find them, you are more of a babysitter than a leader."

I have had many positive experiences that relate to these leadership questions in the course of my last tenure with Canada's largest (nearly 500 stores) service industry franchise, *Canadian Tire*.

During my 19 years as a service manager, a dozen of my staffers went on to be service managers themselves – all of whom served first as assistant managers. One became a general manager, one a national field representative, another became a *Canadian Tire* associate dealer, four of my techs started their independent service outlet, another ex-assistant manager and service manager went on to open his own auto service business, and one staffer went on to be the leading power-train instructor at General Motors. During one of my stints in Calgary, Alberta, one staffer became an assistant manager while another one of my assistants became a service manager and now runs his race car building operation. Numerous other staff moved on to OEMs as well.

My favorite line is, *"If you want a job, I have none to offer, but on the other hand, if you want a career and enjoy this trade, come and spend four years and I'll take you on a journey You will never forget. You will earn more money than you would after four years of university."*

What a Leader Needs to Project

In building a business, leaders must demonstrate a strong work ethic and set the right tone if they want to set an example. The journey of being an effective leader must begin with a peripheral vision and must champion motivation; this determines the path to reach your goals. The journey of leadership teaches a lot. Effective leaders have to master all the smart skill sets that advance their careers. Proactive leaders have to demonstrate they can drive traffic, sales, and consistent profits. You need a savvy mindset and high energy to motivate and challenge staff to become more than they have ever dreamed possible. Leaders will stretch staffers so they can also become career leaders.

A true leader has an apex predator mentality with a confident demeanor but is always willing to show appreciation and respect for each employee by motivating them to work in customers' best interests. If issues arise, they do not attack the offending individuals but rather balance praise and correction. Strong leaders will also praise their staffers in public, repeatedly stand behind them, encourage them, and, when sharing great results, give them all the credit. They will go the extra mile, such as buying pizza for their team outside their existing budget, using their own money, or granting them the favor of leaving a bit early if they need it. The pathway must be clear.

Treat your "internal" customers with the same grace and respect as you would your external ones. Always be a personal model of excellence for your staff.

Leaders must lead with a positive attitude that creates energy, which can be a force multiplier as you conduct your interactions with staff and consumers. This is a long-term strategy. For leaders and front-line cast members who desire and have the passion for advancing and improving their careers, using the resources in this intuitive book will add a new layer and a whole new dimension to your game. Yes, you will be required to put in the work ethic upfront, and soon, the trackable fruit will be visible. You have to show management over some time that you are the next gen-superstar in the making.

Coaching plays a major role at all levels. Bob Bowman was Michael Phelps' swimming coach, who wanted to learn swimming at the age of eleven. Dealing with intentional adversity created by Bowman was a hard lesson to learn. Years later, Michael is known as the most decorated Olympian of all time with a total of twenty-eight Olympic medals, twenty-three of which are gold. He competed in five Olympics, where he was recognized for his formidable butterfly and has now retired as the greatest swimmer of all time. Coaching plays a tremendous role, and I am totally and completely convinced this spectacular book will allow you to achieve and accomplish incredible feats. This book is loaded with industry knowledge to help every frontline cast member excel beyond their wildest dreams. The right coaching, mentoring, and motivation bring further accountability to the entire team. In the automotive service business, we have to constantly practice and rehearse the service moments, keeping a laser focus; it is about re-enforcement time and time again. Similarly, a service manager's job is to coach, educate, and empower the consumer with "What is In It For Me" by sharing the amazing benefits and the incredible value so they feel empowered. Value is what motivates consumers to share their wallets.

"The team you build is the company you build "

–Keith Raboise

"The front line builds your bottom Line"

–Don Funk

"The quality of your customer service will never exceed the quality of the people providing it."

-Liveagent

The question is, how to get your staff to buy in? It begins with more coaching, stronger motivation, and greater accountability. I believe one has to create a new cultural program around recognition by providing a Disney-like environment where par excellence wins the moment and the day. In such dynamics, everyone is inspired and challenged in an educational mindset, where they are equipped with a program that offers a competitive and intellectual ability to launch their career path and then take it to a greater level.

This is what this amazing book provides.

The Takeaway

I believe a necessary leadership trait is to be a dynamic individual. Things often happen very quickly, and one must constantly stay on top of them. One must also develop a motivated, competitive nature that embraces challenges and has a burning desire to win and inspire others. Another key trait is to have a vision and the ability to think and act big, with humility. You must take command and own the room, anticipating the next puzzle piece but always giving the team the full credit. Ultimately, they are the players who get the job done.

Leaders have to be aware of the change and be excellent communicators who think like customers to execute a service experience that exceeds their expectations. This is the secret. Winning is about all the little details.

Leaders need to have their finger on the pulse of the major KPIs: traffic, sales, and profits. They must make the time to coach and mentor individuals so they can grow and polish their skill sets.

In a busy environment, take time to have a "Zoom meeting" to keep staff aware of expectations derived from knowing the statistical effectiveness of each tech and advisor. This requires continual performance measurement. Zoom meetings should also be a time to acknowledge individual accomplishments and be a great encourager. Leaders must be willing to hold staff accountable to high standards and be transparent at all times.

What is the difference between the 20/80 or 25/75 rule where the 20% outperforms the remaining 80%? All the above-mentioned traits which I have alluded to. Take inventory of your skill sets and work on those areas that need attention.

Life is about learning from your experiences. These experiences entail many secrets about how to become a stronger, more effective leader. Your potential is unlimited. Set goals and work on them. The industry needs more great leaders, so be encouraged!

Now that you have come to the end of this dynamic book, hit the switch and throw a brick onto the gas pedal, and get going! And keep doing it every single day, with every single customer, 100% of the time!

Notes

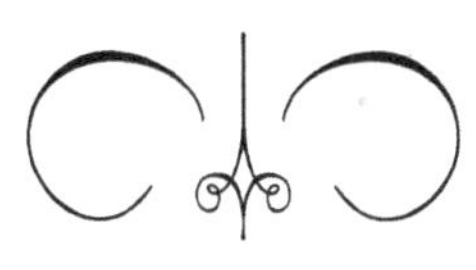

Chapter 13

The Key Secret, The Buck Stops Here

"The Golden Rule for Every Business is this: Put Yourself in Your Customer's Place."

-Orison Swett Marden, American Inspiration Author

A ton of automotive service outlets including O.E.M. dealerships, franchisees/chains, tire shops, and independents struggle with their bottom line or their profit margins. First and foremost, everything must begin with understanding the critical importance of factors that must be followed. These guidelines are a must-follow rule. This financial business model has been around forever. This financial business model is the most critical piece of the puzzle for a solid platform moving forward. Every business line in the P & L needs to be reviewed every year, today inflation must also be at the forefront. However, labor cost is the most critical expense line in your overall expenses. Having the right margins or markup in parts and other supplies is ultra-critical. This is where your focus should be: to begin with hiring people with great character and high I.Q. So often one fails to do the background check over their history years. You quickly learn a lot from following up with their former employer.

There are numerous examples of how to achieve margins. I mean profit formulas that can certainly enhance the bottom-line Profit and Loss statement. In my time as an auto consultant across Canada, I would advise other operators on how to achieve a strong balance sheet, which is the key to greater $uccess. Control labor cost, this is your #1 biggest cost.

My valuable insight will provide you with one example of how to achieve the results that you the operators are seeking. Across the line I have witnessed many great balance sheets; however, the owners need to invest in AI equipment such as Hunter Engineering Autonomous with a quick check drive through. They will love the added value plus the banker would be delighted to give the dollars you may need down the road, i.e. like new equipment and expansion or additional outlet.

A few operators across the board are reflecting a negative balance sheet. The formula below will provide some good guidelines to enhance your operation, so your profits will provide you with a healthy balance sheet, so you have a reasonably comfortable retirement. Let us examine and explore how to achieve better results for whatever your dreams are.

The Formula is as follows, and one can tweak the margins here and there to achieve the desired results. There is a statement, "Business is difficult and uncertain when old habits persist within in today's changing realities" This is also a popular statement that has been around for a long time, it reads:

"If You Cannot Measure It... You Cannot Manage It." This changes your balance sheet/P&L statement. Following is an example of the business model.

The Auto Service Business Model

Without question today's consumers have higher expectations than ever before. Satisfaction is not to be equated with the high bar of excellence. There are some studies that say that 60-70 percent of satisfied customer do not come back and here is why: they are just satisfied.

I want to quote Shep Hyken- "You cannot be satisfactory because satisfactory is a rating—it is right in the middle—it is average—how do you like your haircut—it is fine—fine is like the "F" bomb of customer service. To a lot of people loyalty means we have to keep our customers for life. If we focus on the next time every time ultimately we would create a lifetime of Loyalty."

Here is an alarming stat: A 5% increase in customer loyalty can boost profits by 25 – 90 %. I would call staffers into the office and chat about the importance of delivering the goods. My balance sheet has always generated amazing results. That is what this book is totally about - excellence... make is pop, make it come alive.

We have to refocus our energy on locking in relationships. This higher bar is all about relationship building 100% of the time. If you achieve this, the opportunity of having great benefits is the result. If you want an exceptional relationship, you must consider the long term. Constant upgrading in training is Key, and focusing on leadership while mentoring and investing into your teammates will generate above average performance. One needs to habitually call a brief huddle to say "thanks", but at the same time, inspire and motivate your team to buy into achieving even greater results. Building up people is a skillset; praise is such a powerful tool to have in your toolbox. Use it often to encourage and support your team. Fire up the BBQ, do burgers and for a special touch do up some stakes. Thank your staff for looking after the customer and delivering an outstanding customer experience.

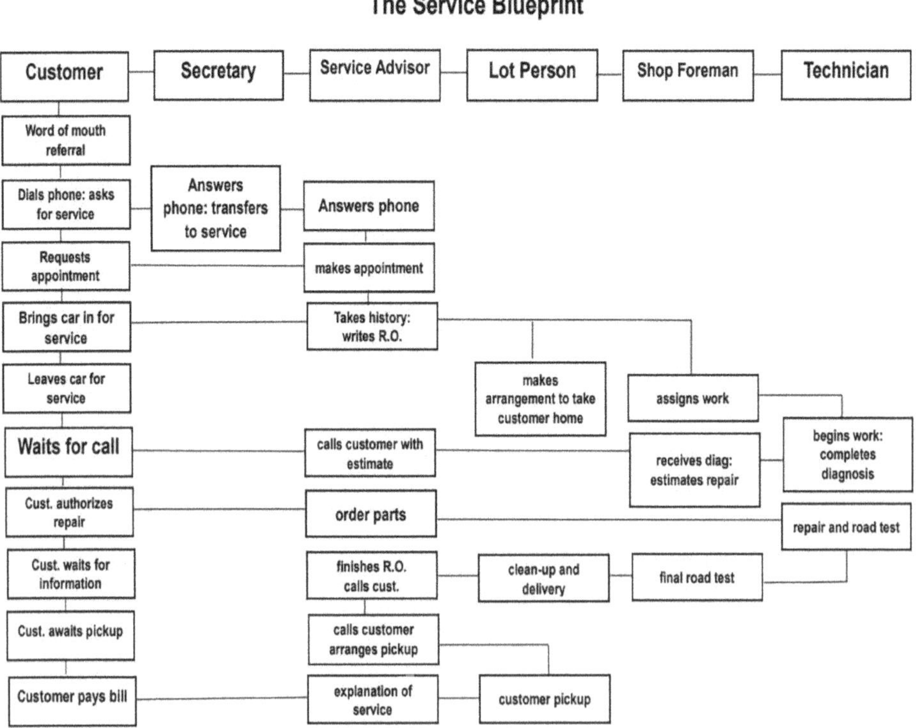

The Auto Service Financial Business Model

At this time I want to draw your attention to what is required to enhance and tweak your Business Model. This will help you understand and maximize tips on how to achieve more profitable margins as they relate to different areas of the Business Model.

Management must have a great understanding of each of the expense lines. It is critical to understand how to manage the cost of parts versus the right margins. Likewise, the owner needs to negotiate added discounts from suppliers based on volume; it never hurts to ask.

Parts Margins:

Parts includes all the obvious inventory costs. On small parts you should or could mark up the percentage to achieve a little more margin. On larger parts you might want to mark them up slightly more to achieve the right margins. Warranty is another factor to consider. Hazmat are the hazardous materials used to clean up parts. Sanding materials and sprays are required to free the movement of certain components to allow them to function more readily. These hazardous materials need to be handled under certain protocols. In some jurisdictions these hazardous materials are part of the shop supplies. In others, shop supplies need to be broken down as a separate cost line. Wheel weights are needed to balance tires which also could be billed out on a separate cost line; some may choose to include them in shop supplies. Lubrication and welding rods are needed to resurface certain parts. There are different ways of handling cost related materials. Certain operators eat the cost, which I would not recommend. I believe service advisors need to understand and share and explain these products to the consumers so that the consumers have a clear understanding of what is involved. Open communications make consumers feel they have been informed. The rule of thumb margins should be in the 35 - 40 % range; some operators look at even slightly higher margins.

Labor Margins:

Labor sales are minus the cost. The cost will change from region to region. Another cost one has to factor into the equation is worker's compensation, insurance, holidays/vacation, allowance for sick days, training, etc. Labor margins are affected more by shop productivity than by your actual labor cost, sometimes referred to as the "door rate". Inflation needs to be factored in on a yearly basis. And to keep your team in place one needs to adjust the hourly labor cost according to the specific market place. I believe in annual personnel reviews. This is often overlooked, and with today's staff shortage one needs to stay on top of these concerns. Sometimes these cost increases need to be factored in which may require the adjustment of the charge out rate.

The wage cost needs to be controlled to be within the 30 to 33 percent range.

ARO:

The ARO reflects the average repair order. In today's market place I am a strong believer in being disciplined to do a digital vehicle inspection on every single vehicle. This is an amazing tool that can inform and educate the consumer via pictures or videos. This can be sent to the consumers, via text or emails, and sometimes a follow up conversation needs to take place. It is all about informing and educating the consumer. Sometimes consumers are aware of certain repairs their vehicle may need, but doing a full digital vehicle inspection will make sure the vehicle is road worthy. Thus no surprises. I see too many cases where the basic disciplines are short cutted or simply ignored. These are killers to one's business. ARO is a benchmark based on the mix of vehicle models and age. Bay capacity is a key factor.

Shop Productivity by Techs:

This is simply the number of hours billed out versus the number of hours on the floor on any given day. Another element in dealing with productivity is determined by smoke breaks, time on the phone, length of coffee breaks and their work ethics. Some techs do not always bill all their times. This should not be the case. Encourage excellence within your group. The key is great customer satisfaction. The daily car count impacts the average repair order.

Gross Profit Margins:

Gross margins should be measured on a daily, weekly, and monthly basis. Car Count X ARO X AGM = GPM (Gross Profit margins). I would calculate my monthly sales and be able to ball park what the margins would be before the accounting was done. The percentage from gross margins to profits should be in the 30 to 40 range. The more productive shops could certainly reach the 50% mark.

Profits:

Profit is the key factor. It is all about controlling all your costs while delivering a 5-Star performance to a "T". It is a process of controlling the costs. I was blessed to have high margins, profit wise. It is about executing all of the little details. Profits should be in the 20 to 30% mark. When you work smart at cost control and exercise all the disciplines noted in this book, that profit number will be beyond your imagination. It can be done.

The Auto Service Business Model:

Parts Margins	35 to 50%
Labor Margins:	33 to 35%
ARO:	$340 or five times labor rate or 2.5 to 3 hours per repair order is an average
Gross Profit Margins:	35% to 55%
Nets Profits:	20% to 30% well managed stores can reach the high 30%

This GENESES and POWERFUL masterpiece Book defines the quality of service that each client will receive. This service blueprint experience will attract new acquisitions, it will generate constant retention, and this is about the moment of truth. The important thing to remember is that walking on water is easy if you know where the rocks are. This book will teach you how to understand service by opening your eyes and mind, it is a series of events that the whole team must embrace and execute 100% of the time, always be amazing. No tools, systems, processes or platforms will ever replace meticulous attention to detail. The service blueprint is a simple matter of documenting each and every service event in terms of what is happening and who is involved. See "The Service Blueprint" in chapter #13. That is why every service agent who interacts with a consumer needs this powerful book, it is great "on boarding" tool and empowering handbook, to assist you in reaching the level of excellence. Visit: donfunkofficalbookwebsite.com This is a $UCCESS manual that will encourage you to implement new ideas and strategies. The word "Killer" refers to better servicing the customer, better equipping the staff to becoming more for the right reasons, and killing it with better execution of the disciplines. All of these combined will step up your operation for great growth and better success.

EPILOGUE

I have always believed in the pursuit of a worthy goal of excellence; if something is worth doing, do it so well that you gain a reputation for it. Five amazing decades in the auto service industry have broadened my experience and taught me to continue to create the desire and passion for delivering above and beyond. It has to be about one person, the customer, and their experience; so embrace, equip, engage, educate, and execute. Engaging every consumer with the formula should lead to a special event by transforming, celebrating, and making the customer service experience like that of going to a Disney Theme Park.

I understood very early in my five decades of career in the auto service industry that consumers have very high expectations from their service providers, and rightfully so. If you desire to grow your business, you need to step up your customer service game. Your goal in life should be about challenging yourself and your team to deliver an amazing experience to the consumer, so they light up the social media sites to share their enthusiastic experience.

Customer service experience must be above and beyond; it must begin with detailing and focusing on each of the steps so that each interaction is concise and precise. Map out the process, starting by welcoming your guests or VIPs (very important people), as this drives the business. The guests are willing to share their wallets when you deliver a personalized process; this can be done by exercising your memory muscles and making an effort to remember their names all the while being exceptionally helpful.

In the end, the guests acknowledge staffers who are professional, relevant, and authentic. The service providers need to learn to internalize these steps in every interaction while delivering a flawless and seamless experience. This investment rules the day and leads to double-digit exponential growth. It is the power of consistently delivering an impactful and meaningful customer service experience since it is the number one driver of sales. Your customer service should be of high priority. By investing in all the front-line staffers' soft skill sets, you can deliver a 'Wow!' experience, where you own the service moment.

Furthermore, you need to be proud and bold about soliciting powerful feedback by stating on your repair invoice, *"We would love to hear about your experience. Please visit www.osf.ca (or whatever manner the corporation has chosen) and fill out a guest feedback form or follow the QR Code."*

Secondly, you must constantly invest in your cast members to help them develop their skills and careers. Take every opportunity and make it a teaching moment; if done right, it is the greatest ROI.

As a team leader, you need to have a passion for coaching, mentoring, stretching, challenging, motivating, encouraging, instilling accountability, and trusting the process. Enhancing development is about drilling down and expanding on the soft skill sets, which are considered as smart and powerful skills. It is about the constant work to refine all the processes of the industry. An example is when you quit the pushy sales approach and start to educate consumers about the amazing benefits and the incredible value, thus, empowering the consumer to the level where they sell themselves. It can be boiled down to using smart processes with the choice and usage of the right industry language.

It is always about shaping the consumer's mindset whereby they understand "What is in it for me?" Consumers want value; That is what motivates them to be willing to share their wallets without the grudge of purchase and makes them willing to express their positive experiences on all the various channels of social media. The reviews result in referrals to their family, friends, and associates to shift their loyalty, while in essence, they become an evangelist of your brand. That is the power of return on investment in staffers.

The game-changer that provides further impact is an investment in smart devices, such as Hunter Engineering Quick Check Drive, which is an effortless wheel alignment system that generates a colorful document of steering inspection within seconds. The green color on the document indicates the vehicle is within the manufacturer's spec, which creates that third-party-neutral assessment. The red-colored wheel, on the other hand, indicates that the vehicle alignment is outside of the manufacturer's specs and needs attention.

In the testimonials from Hunter Engineering, their clients share this rich content, whereby their customers increased their wheel alignments by 300% and paid off the amazing Quick Check Drive alignment tool in the first three months.

In my career as a service manager, 12 years ago, consumers purchased 4086 wheel alignments. While consulting and using this great investment in one service center, new alignments jumped by 500%, further maximizing the return on investment. As an option, one can also have an autonomous tread depth inspection done which will capture each groove of the tires and print the readings in the form of a color document. The analytic data reveals that 3 out of every 10 vehicles will require a set of tires. The data continues to strongly indicate that the first service provider to bring this information to the consumer's mindset will be rewarded with 70% of these consumers' buy-in.

DVI captures all the inspection items. The pictures and videos supported with industry language help educate the consumer in real-time, along with third-party evidence, and can easily be viewed using a tablet or a smartphone. In the event the consumer is at work, at home, or running errands, they can immediately receive a text and in turn, communicate back and forth. The consumers can see virtually, with confidence and comfort, the evidence and the digital inspection report which provides extra added value to help them understand a safety concern or make the choice about the repair or replacement of a necessary item. Seeing their vehicle components in their current state becomes the game-changer, and in the future, consumers will gravitate to auto repair centers that use these devices, which provide added value and you will be assured of hearing a lot more "Yes" to the process of keeping them and their family safe while seeing the advantage of saving money and time.

Investment in technology is experiencing record-breaking results. However, some believe it is a cost they cannot justify. Times are changing rapidly, and you cannot afford to let technology pass you by. Hunter Engineering and AutoServe1 provide a win-win that will change your life.

These amazing and stunning smart investments mimic what most service agents cannot always express, as pictures and videos provide neutral third-party evidence in real time. These reports are game-changers. These smart devices allow consumers to fall in love with these high-tech insights, which they will expect and want going forward. These stunning vehicle reports raise trust by empowering the consumers. Like they say, *"That is a no-brainer."*

The financial business model strongly supports the empirical evidence that, yes, it is an initial cost. However, it can be recovered within three to eight months, depending on bay size and annual traffic, with a significant return on investment. The impact supports the <u>three</u> major KPIs: traffic, sales, and profit. The focus needs to be on new acquisitions, driven by higher retention (your consumer CSI) thus increasing loyalty, increased higher average repair tickets, resulting in greater profits. It is an investment, not a cost, and a more positive and stronger indicator of the growth cycle. The biggest room within the auto service industry is the room for greater improvement. This book is all about that. Times are changing more rapidly than we think. Our biggest obstacles are what I refer to as breaking out of that "comfort zone." You have got to put in the work, first and foremost. What we celebrate, That is what continues to grow!

If you break down the phrase "Stepping out of your comfort zone," it means doing things that you don›t feel comfortable doing and getting out of your comfort level is a must. I encourage you to push yourself into unfamiliar places and to do things that you wouldn't normally do. It is also defined as "A behavioral state within a person which operates in an anxiety-neutral condition, using a limited set of behaviors to deliver a steady level of low performance."

I had to constantly challenge myself while writing and compiling this book; I did not realize the tremendous amount of time, energy, and work it would take. My challenge was for the impossible to become the possible; writing about the possibility of living my dream to explore and share insights while looking at all the metrics that were needed to re-elevate the customer service experience in the automotive industry. I have drilled down into all the critical elements that are the key drivers, chapter by chapter, that focus on change in delivering new insights by taking every metric and breaking it down using artificial intelligence and smart devices and supporting them with financial business models, which are eye-opening.

The content of this book is the greatest general source of industry insight, as industry analytics, artificial intelligence, smart devices, developed financial business models, and combined new and advanced technology were used. It includes insights, concepts, and new ideas to write and provide valuable and rich content, which needs to be in the hands of the CEO, general manager, op's manager, service manager, and every front-line service advisor, which will create a Disney-like over-the-top experience with the help of social media to create a win for the consumer. The concepts of this book will transform your auto service business model going forward; some shops are there already. I believe others will adopt these brilliant insights to control their future by having a firm grasp of the killer instinct, to become more by doing more. I know this book has an award-winning potential to help you drive your business, your career, and your future to a greater $uccess. This is what the top thinkers are doing. They are constantly thinking bigger. There is a plethora of opportunities inside these pages. With the investment in this masterpiece, it will be a refresher course to get the juices flowing, to press in more, to engage in an attitude that you can become invincible. This is an ROI book.

Without question, each of the chapters brings powerful insights to the operation to generate a constant double-digit growth. To sum it all up, I have researched, explored, and applied the effects and impact of Hunter Engineering and AutoServ1; I have listened to the testimonials that provided clear statements about the unbelievable results that changed fortunes. These are real because I have used and implemented their well-thought-out processes and best practices.

Here is a John Quiney quote:

"If your actions inspire others to dream more, learn more, do more, and become more, you are a Leader."

And Andrew Carnegie says:

"Teamwork: the fuel that allows common people to attain uncommon results."

NOTES

Appendix

This section contains permission letters and acknowledgments from the respective sources.

For Chapter 3 (Delloite US):

Mackin, Rory <rmackin@DELOITTE.com>
Mon 2021-03-08 8:21 AM

To:

- You

Don, thanks for checking, feel free to use this publicly available piece giving any credits to Deloitte as appropriate.

Contact Deloitte US

Please find the details below:

- first:Don
- second:Funk
- email:d.e.funk@hotmail.com
- companyname:Don Funk Auto Consulting
- jobtitle:President
- phonenumber:306-221-7784
- zip:S7V1K7
- location:CA
- yourmessage:In regards to your article: "Becoming irresistible: A new model for employee engagement" - Deloitte Review Issue 16 -
I am writing a book on the auto service industry - vehicle repair side - and am herewith requesting permission to use this article - in whole or in part - and will provide credits.
The industry is in the old school mode - I strongly believe that a new model for employment engagement is a must have in today's society.
Looking forward to an early reply. Thank you in advance for your assistance in this matter.
- emailconsent:yes
- privacystatement:item1
- dunsnumber:
- uid:
- TopicDropdown:Services
- FormReferenceId:{ec95d5b3919b34278e9a48699cbf29c6fb5f47a59da0703e91511fae755aa72ed8a45cc3eaef8a11f27be277c9bbdd34641aaaefe04d4954a0d414b50121bb777893384fb1b81449a12fcd9a415f42a7126b4692cd038421bd9efa923ff3abae6f5bd0f79cd3e2102a77fd736fb851de}

Chapters 6 and 7 (Jamie Cuthbert):

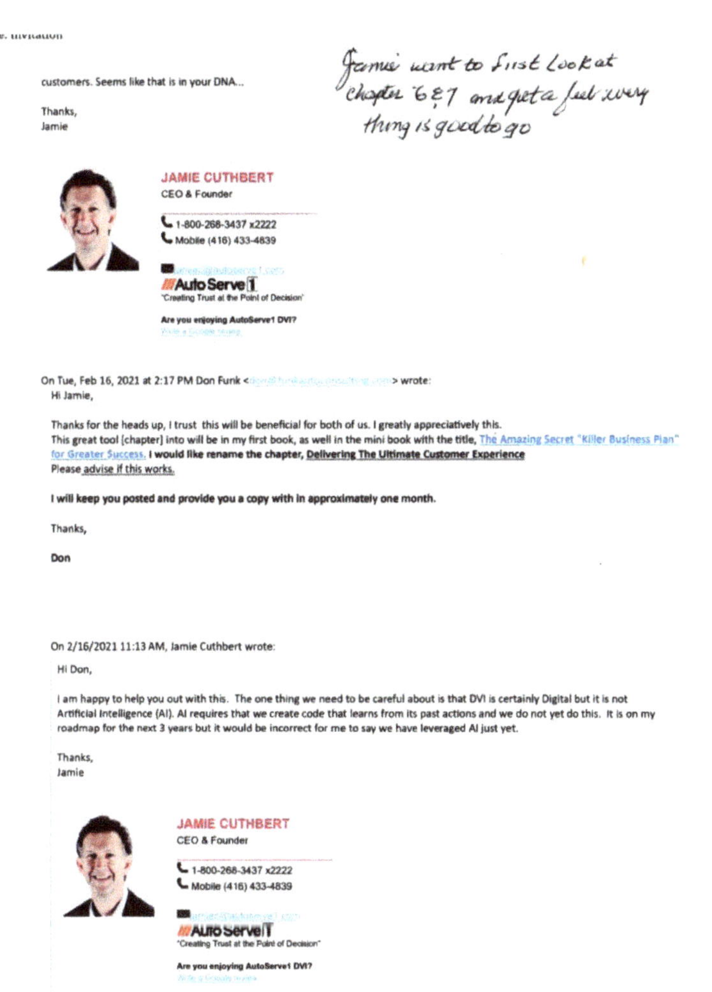

customers. Seems like that is in your DNA...

Thanks,
Jamie

Jamie want to first look at chapter 6 & 7 and get a feel every thing is good to go

JAMIE CUTHBERT
CEO & Founder

1-800-268-3437 x2222
Mobile (416) 433-4839

AutoServe1
"Creating Trust at the Point of Decision"

Are you enjoying AutoServe1 DVI?

On Tue, Feb 16, 2021 at 2:17 PM Don Funk <> wrote:

Hi Jamie,

Thanks for the heads up, I trust this will be beneficial for both of us. I greatly appreciatively this.
This great tool [chapter] into will be in my first book, as well in the mini book with the title, The Amazing Secret "Killer Business Plan" for Greater Success. **I would like rename the chapter, Delivering The Ultimate Customer Experience**
Please advise if this works.

I will keep you posted and provide you a copy with in approximately one month.

Thanks,

Don

On 2/16/2021 11:13 AM, Jamie Cuthbert wrote:

Hi Don,

I am happy to help you out with this. The one thing we need to be careful about is that DVI is certainly Digital but it is not Artificial Intelligence (AI). AI requires that we create code that learns from its past actions and we do not yet do this. It is on my roadmap for the next 3 years but it would be incorrect for me to say we have leveraged AI just yet.

Thanks,
Jamie

JAMIE CUTHBERT
CEO & Founder

1-800-268-3437 x2222
Mobile (416) 433-4839

AutoServe1
"Creating Trust at the Point of Decision"

Are you enjoying AutoServe1 DVI?

! of 6 2/27/2021, 6:24 PM

Chapter 8 (Hunter Engineering Co.):

TEL (314) 731-3020 FAX (314) 716-1355

11250 Hunter Drive
Bridgeton, Missouri 63044-2391 U.S.A.

http://www.hunter.com
e-mail: info@hunter.com

January 27, 2021

Mr. Don Funk
806 Bellmont Crescent
Saskatoon, SK. S7V1K7
CANADA

Re: Publication of Hunter Engineering Co. advertising and website materials.

Dear Mr. Funk,

I have reviewed your letter to Mr. Brauer, together with the draft of Chapter 20 "Winning Big With Hunter Engineering" from the manuscript you are currently preparing. Thank you for providing us with an opportunity to review the draft and to inquire about the use of our website, advertising materials, and product literature in your book.

The materials from our website and advertising brochures is protected by copyright laws. Hunter Engineering Co. hereby grants you permission to include and utilize Hunter Engineering Co. information and materials from our public website and product literature in your manuscript, subject to the following restrictions:

(1) Any information and material from the Hunter Engineering Co. website and/or product literature which you choose to use shall not be altered or modified (resizing to fit within page margins, direct quotes, etc. are permissible).

(2) A statement identifying Hunter Engineering Co. as the source of the information shall be included with the materials. e.g. "Used with permission from Hunter Engineering Co."

If you have any questions regarding this approval, you may direct them to my attention by e-mail to MBooks@Hunter.com. I wish you the best success with your publication, and look forward to seeing the end result.

Sincerely,

/ Mark E. Books /

Intellectual Property Counsel
Hunter Engineering Co.

Chapter 11 (AskPatty.com Inc.):

Message-ID: <CAK5ZnbcMdpK6u4z3zuYVickbuE7QYf+0OMPAG8X48+0gv7yasQ@mail.gmail.com>
Content-Type: multipart/related; boundary="000000000000f99fb305bbb7610e"
X-Spam-Status: No, score=-1.4
X-Spam-Score: -13
X-Spam-Bar: -
X-Ham-Report: Spam detection software, running on the system "ca1.beagle.io", has NOT identified this incoming email as spam. The original message has been attached to this so you can view it or label similar future email. If you have any questions, see root\@localhost for details. Content preview: Don, You have quite a story, congrats! Yes, go ahead and use the info on the article just be sure to "credit" AskPatty.com and myself. Best Regards, Content analysis details: (-1.4 points, 5.0 required) pts rule name description ---- ---------------------- -- -1.9 BAYES_00 BODY: Bayes spam probability is 0 to 1% [score: 0.0011] 0.0 URIBL_BLOCKED ADMINISTRATOR NOTICE: The query to URIBL was blocked. See http://wiki.apache.org/spamassassin/DnsBlocklists#dnsbl-block for more information. [URIs: certifiedfemalefriendly.com] 0.0 HTML_MESSAGE BODY: HTML included in message 0.1 DKIM_SIGNED Message has a DKIM or DK signature, not necessarily valid -0.1 DKIM_VALID Message has at least one valid DKIM or DK signature 0.5 KAM_NUMSUBJECT Subject ends in numbers excluding current years
X-Spam-Flag: NO

Don,

You have quite a story, congrats! Yes, go ahead and use the info on the article just be sure to "credit" AskPatty.com and myself.

Best Regards,

Jody DeVere
CEO
AskPatty.com, Inc.
www.askpatty.com

PH: 888-737-8599 x 6
Cell : 805-208-1008
Fax: 805- 435-2609
eMail: jdevere@askpatty.com
Twitter: http://twitter.com/askpatty

AskPatty.com Certified Female Friendly®
www.certifiedfemalefriendly.com

https://encrypted-tbn0.gstatic.com/images?q=tbn:ANd9GcQu95lA1NzHxPkkstL1LkBZF8y9Yw-acW9X6go4FaoaIVeXjCRb

www.ingramcontent.com/pod-product-compliance
Lightning Source LLC
Chambersburg PA
CBHW051137120626
46547CB00012B/833

9781963209310